FLAVOURS OF ORIGIN

AN INSIGHT ON PURCHASE OF GI PRODUCTS OF KERALA

DR. MANOJ M
DR. A SULEKHA

Contents

Acknowledgements

"It shall be the duty of every citizen of India to develop the scientific temper, humanism and the spirit of inquiry and reform."

- Article 51A(h) of the Indian Constitution

This thesis, a part of my doctoral degree, was possible only with the guidance and support of many people. I take this privilege to acknowledge the contribution of many individuals who have been inspirational and supportive throughout my work, and who have most importantly endowed me with knowledge. It is an outcome of continuous help and inspiration from many eminent personalities and soulful individuals who directly and indirectly supported me for my successful Ph.D thesis completion. I hereby place on record the support, encouragement and motivation extended to me by my teachers, family and friends during the course of my research.

First and foremost, I thank my guide and Research Supervisor **Dr. A. SULEKHA**, Head and Assistant Professor, Department of Commerce and Research, V.L.B. Janakiammal College of Arts and Science (Autonomous), for her valuable guidance and moral support rendered at every phase of my study. Her constructive guidance and relentless support helped me alot in completing my work successfully in time. She is a constant source of knowledge and inspiration with loving and caring attitude. Without her guidance and support professionally and personally my thesis wouldn't have been completed.

I am highly obliged to the Respondents of various Districts of Kerala for their timely response and co-operation. I am highly indebted to them for the patience they have shown in sharing their opinion. Their extensive knowledge, practical suggestions and even constructive criticisms were extremely useful for my research work.

I run short of words when it comes to thank my Parents, for their abundant love, care and support rendered to claim the ladders of success throughout my life and also for being a pillar at every step in my personal and academic life.

My heartfelt gratitude to Friends and Well-wishers for standing besides me through these tiring times, an indispensable part of research. I am extremely grateful to them for their endless encouragement, love and support.

Contents

Foreword

In today's globalized marketplace, consumers are inundated with choices. From the shelves of supermarkets to the digital storefronts of e-commerce platforms, the options seem endless. In such a landscape, how does one decide what to purchase? What influences our buying decisions, and how can we make informed choices that align with our values and preferences?

The concept of Geographical Indications (GIs) has emerged as a significant factor in shaping consumer behavior. GIs denote products with a specific geographical origin and possess qualities, reputation, or characteristics that are essentially attributable to that place of origin. Think of Champagne from France, Parmigiano-Reggiano from Italy, or Darjeeling tea from India. These products carry with them a story, a tradition, and a sense of authenticity that resonate with consumers.

The Impact of Geographical Indication Labeling on Consumer Buying Behavior is a comprehensive exploration into this fascinating intersection of geography, culture, and consumerism. In this book, the authors delve into the multifaceted dynamics at play when consumers encounter products labeled with GIs. Through meticulous research and insightful analysis, they unravel the complexities of how geographical indications influence consumer perceptions, preferences, and ultimately, purchasing decisions.

As you embark on this journey through the pages of this book, you will gain a deeper understanding of the profound influence that geographical indications exert on the choices we make as consumers. Whether you are a scholar, a practitioner in the field of marketing or trade, or simply a curious individual interested in the intricacies of consumer behavior, this book offers valuable insights that will enrich your understanding of the modern marketplace.

I commend the authors for their dedication and expertise in bringing this subject to light. Their work represents a significant contribution to the literature on consumer behavior and the role of geographical indications in shaping global commerce. May this book serve as a catalyst for further exploration and dialogue in this vital area of study.

Dr. Matilda Danny

H.O.D

P.G Department of Commerce

Yuvakshetra Institute of Management Studies

Mundur

Preface

In a world where globalization has interconnected economies and cultures more than ever before, understanding the factors that influence consumer behavior is paramount. Among these factors, the Impact of Geographical Indication (GI) labeling on consumer buying behavior stands out as a significant area of study. As consumers navigate an increasingly complex marketplace, products bearing geographical indications offer a unique promise of authenticity, tradition, and quality tied to their specific places of origin.

This book seeks to explore the intricate relationship between geographical indication labeling and consumer buying behavior. It stems from a recognition of the profound implications that GIs have on consumer perceptions and preferences, and the far-reaching consequences for producers, traders, policymakers, and consumers themselves.

The chapters within this book are the culmination of extensive research, rigorous analysis, and insightful observations from scholars and practitioners across various disciplines. From examining the psychological mechanisms underlying consumer responses to GIs to exploring the economic implications for producers and regions, each chapter offers a nuanced perspective on the multifaceted impact of geographical indication labeling.

We delve into the rich tapestry of case studies spanning diverse products and regions, providing illuminating insights into the varying dynamics at play. Whether it's the preservation of traditional craftsmanship in rural communities or the strategic positioning of products in global markets, the implications of geographical indication labeling reverberate across industries and geographies.

As editors, our aim is to present a comprehensive overview of this complex subject, bridging theoretical insights with practical implications for stakeholders in the global marketplace. We invite readers to engage with the diverse perspectives presented in this book, fostering a deeper understanding of the intricate interplay between geographical indications and consumer behavior.

Ultimately, our hope is that this book serves as a valuable resource for scholars, policymakers, industry professionals, and anyone interested in unraveling the mysteries of consumer decision-making in an increasingly interconnected world.

Dr. Manoj M

CHAPTER I

INTRODUCTION

1. GEOGRAPHICAL INDICATION

Geographical Indication (GI) serves as a distinctive marker that indicates the origin of a particular product from a specific geographical area. It signifies that the product possesses certain qualities, reputation, or other distinctive characteristics that can be primarily attributed to its geographical origin. Therefore, the primary purpose of a geographical indication (GI) is to establish a correlation between the specific attributes, qualities, or reputation of a product and its geographical origin. Geographical indications (GIs) are primarily employed for agricultural and food commodities, which commonly exhibit a strong inherent association with their specific geographical location. Nevertheless, there are also numerous geographical indications (GIs) associated with various other types of commodities. The distinctive attributes of the product may be attributed to conventional manufacturing expertise or a synergistic blend of indigenous knowledge and available natural resources. Producers are exclusively authorised to utilise geographical indications, provided that their goods adhere to the relevant criteria pertaining to the product's origin, processing method, and characteristic attributes. The utilisation of protected indications is restricted for production sites situated beyond the geographical area of origin and for goods that fail to comply with the relevant requirements. At both National and Regional levels, Geographical Indications (GIs) are safeguarded through a diverse range of legal mechanisms. Included in these legal frameworks are sui generis systems of laws that are specifically crafted to safeguard geographical indications, typically through the implementation of a registration process. Sui generis systems typically offer safeguards against both direct and indirect commercial exploitation of geographical indications (GI), as well as protection against any attempts to imitate them. Sui generis systems for geographical indication (GI) protection are implemented in numerous countries, as well as by two regional intergovernmental entities, namely the African Intellectual Property Organisation (OAPI) and the European Union (EU). In the context of India, the safeguarding of products through Geographical Indications has been linked to specific concerns and obstacles. The thesis aims to elucidate the various factors that exert an influence on consumer behaviour

pertaining to Geographical Indication (GI) products. The purchasing behaviour of consumers is influenced by a multitude of factors that impact the decision-making process. These factors include physical pleasure, the income effect, the price effect, reference groups, culture, social class, product choice, brand and store selection, purchase timing and amount, perception, and post-purchase behaviour, among others. The interdependence of various factors and their impact on consumer decision-making are evident. The acquisition of a geographical indication is determined by the consumer's proximity to the location, their engagement with tourism destinations, the utilisation of various information sources, individual perspectives, and varying levels of satisfaction based on prior experiences. Therefore, the purchase decision is contingent on numerous factors. These factors may have a direct correlation with products.

2. OVERVIEW OF GEOGRAPHICAL INDICATION AND ITS SIGNIFICANCE

Geographical Indications (GI) refer to a type of intellectual property that serves to designate a product's origin from a distinct geographical area while also signifying specific qualities, characteristics, or reputation that are inherently associated with that particular region. Geographical indications (GIs) have the potential to be utilised in various sectors, including agriculture, handicrafts, and industry, encompassing products that possess a distinct association with a particular geographic region. Several products that are safeguarded by Geographical Indications (GI) include Champagne, Roquefort cheese, Darjeeling tea, and Colombian coffee. The importance of geographical indications (GIs) resides in their capacity to safeguard the reputation and excellence of products that possess distinctiveness associated with a specific geographical area. Legal protection is afforded to producers in order to safeguard them from unfair competition and imitation, thereby instilling consumer confidence in the authenticity and superior quality of the products they are purchasing. Consequently, this phenomenon fosters economic growth and the preservation of cultural heritage while also providing assistance to small-scale and traditional producers. In addition to affording legal safeguards, geographical indications (GIs) can serve as a strategic marketing instrument, facilitating product differentiation within a saturated market and endorsing the distinctive attributes associated with a specific geographical area. This phenomenon has the potential to ultimately result in heightened sales and revenue for producers, thereby making a significant contribution to overall economic development.

GIs enjoy protection under various international agreements, including the Agreement on Trade-Related Aspects of Intellectual Property Rights (TRIPS), and are acknowledged by numerous nations globally. The acquisition of geographical indication (GI) protection can be a multifaceted undertaking that necessitates the demonstration of the distinctive attributes of the product alongside the verification of its production within a designated geographical area in accordance with established methodologies or traditions. Nevertheless, the advantages of geographical indication (GI) protection render it a valuable investment for numerous producers and organisations.

3. HISTORY OF GI PROTECTION IN INDIA

The origins of geographical indication (GI) protection in India can be traced back to the early 20th century. The Madras Chamber of Commerce and Industry put forth the initial proposal for the protection of geographical indications in India in 1905. There has been a suggestion to grant legal protection to specific regions in order to safeguard the distinctive characteristics of their products. Nevertheless, the enactment of the Geographical Indications of Goods (Registration and Protection) Act by the Indian government occurred in 1999. The legislation facilitates the registration of geographical indications (GIs) for products that originate from a particular geographic region and possess distinctive qualities, reputations, or other distinguishing characteristics. The process of registering a Geographical Indication (GI) in India entails the submission of an application to the Geographical Indications Registry, situated in Chennai. Since the enactment of the aforementioned legislation, a number of products have been officially recognised and registered as Geographical Indications (GIs) in the country of India. These products include Darjeeling Tea, Banarasi Sarees, Pashmina Shawls, and Alphonso Mangoes. The legislation has additionally served to safeguard the welfare of rural communities engaged in the production of these goods, affording them legal safeguards against the unauthorised exploitation or misappropriation of their traditional knowledge.

In summary, India possesses a comprehensive legal framework that effectively safeguards geographical indications. The implementation of Geographical Indication (GI) protection has played a significant role in both promoting and safeguarding the distinct

identity and cultural heritage associated with diverse products. Simultaneously, it has also made substantial contributions to the economic advancement of rural communities engaged in the production of these goods.

4. GEOGRAPHICAL INDICATION AND KERALA

Kerala, a state located in the southwestern region of India, is positioned along the tropical Malabar Coast, encompassing a coastline of approximately 600 kilometres along the Arabian Sea. Kerala, often referred to as "God's Own Country," boasts a rich historical background encompassing art, cultural heritage, and extensive foreign trade relations with various nations. The tropical climate, coupled with the bountiful monsoon, contributes to the picturesque landscapes of the region. Additionally, the ample presence of water bodies, including numerous rivers and extensive coastlines, further enhances the overall allure of the area. Thiruvananthapuram, historically regarded as the capital city, has long been recognised as a prominent and highly recommended destination. The state is characterised by the Western Ghats, a mountain range renowned for its tea, coffee, and spice plantations, as well as its diverse wildlife. As of the present time, Kerala has obtained a total of 36 Geographical Indication (GI) Tags for its various products. The most recent additions to this list include Agricultural Products such as Attappady Attukombu Avara (beans), Attappady Thuvara (red gramme), Onattukara Ellu (sesame), Kanthalloor-Vattavada

Veluthulli (garlic), and Kodungalloor Pottuvellari (snap melon). These products have successfully obtained Geographical Indications, with the certificate of registration being received on December 21, 2022.

5. SIGNIFICANCE OF THE STUDY

This study holds substantial legal and economic importance as it investigates the various factors that influence consumer behaviour towards Geographical Indication (GI) Products, thereby contributing to their developmental support. This study provides academics with the opportunity to conduct an analysis in the field of Geographical indications. The majority of research studies on the contribution of Geographical indications to development have been conducted in the European Union (EU) and various developing countries.

The objective of this study is to ascertain the factors that customers prioritise and their impact on purchase frequency and price paid. The study additionally examines the variations in consumer behaviour across gender and income cohorts. The primary objective of this study is to assist manufacturers and sellers of GI Products in the State of Kerala in comprehending the specific preferences and purchasing behaviours of their customers.

6. STATEMENT OF THE PROBLEM

The importance of Geographical Indication has put on the forefront in international trade, because socioeconomic and development potentials are associated with registered Geographical Indications. Through Geographical Indication registration of the product, producers get right to forbid any unlawful use, usurpation or fake use of name or sign on a product which is not from geographical indication designated area or which does not have unique qualities that guaranteed through Geographical Indication Protection.

Based on the issues focused following questions are raised by the researcher for analysis and assessment of data:

- What is the demographic status of Geographical Indication Product consumers (sample respondents) ?
- What are the factors that influence the consumer buying behavior of Geographical Indication Products ?
- What impact does the Geographical Indication Labeling creates and how it influence the purchase behaviour?
- What is the Level of satisfaction after the consumption of Geographical Indication Products ?

CHAPTER II

REVIEW OF LITERATURE

INTRODUCTION

The literature review is the most important element of the dissertation, since it serves as the foundation for further research and future studies. The examination of literature allows the researcher to identify and to restrict the research issue. The literature review provides a more in-depth grasp of previous research and a clear explanation of the problem. The examination of literature highlights excellent works and supports the researcher in identifying research needs.

A literature review assists the researcher in establishing expertise in the specific field of study and determining the essential aspects related to the research topic. Finally, the literature review connects to prior results and aids the researcher in evaluating the study.

The chapter discusses the numerous literatures linked with this research; the literature review gives in-depth knowledge on geographical indication, factors influencing purchase of GI Products, Buying behaviour, Problems and Challenges of Geographical Indication Products.

REVIEW OF LITREATURE

Prathap & C.C., (2022) 1 The point Consumers often have trouble deciding whether or not to buy traditional handloom clothing because they don't have any information that would help them judge the quality of the item. The fact that there are more and more fake goods on the market adds to the lack of knowledge. The goal of the study is to find out what makes people want to buy traditional handloom clothes with Geographical Indication (GI) certification, which follows the rules set by the World Intellectual Property Organisation (WIPO) for certification. What we found the results show that quality awareness has a good effect on product diagnosticity, which is helped by the GI label approval. This, in turn, makes perceived information imbalance less of a problem. Also, it was found that a decrease in perceived information imbalance made people more likely to buy traditional handloom clothing. This effect was fully mediated by perceived quality and product trust. Limitations/implications of the research Customers who want to buy traditional handlooms but don't know much about them will benefit from the GI approval label, which verifies the quality of the product's characteristics. The study showed that product diagnosticity (through GI certification) could lower perceived information imbalance, which leads to the consumer's view of quality and trust in the product, which makes the consumer want to buy traditional handloom clothing. The results of the study can help come up with marketing plans to get a bigger share of the market.

Ahmed & Kamble (2022)2 tries to find out what is going on with the registered goods in the state of Maharashtra. The registered goods come from three different categories: agriculture, arts and handicrafts, and manufactured products. Most of these goods are farming, and fruits make up the biggest part of the agricultural group. The study looked at all the goods that have been recorded since the Act went into effect. The paper talks about how the listed Geographical Indications of the Maharashtra State are doing right now. Since the Geographical Indications of Goods (Registration and Protection) Act, 1999, went into effect in 1999, 34 items or goods have been registered with the Government of India. In this study, the writers look at the data they've gathered based on what kind of object it is, where it was registered, and when it was registered. Geographical marking has also been talked about in terms of its meaning, purpose, background, and origins. The author also names some of the goods that are not on the GI register or have not been listed.

Glogovețan et al., (2022)3 It has been found that food, agriculture, and labelling all have an impact on the environment, and that the balance between these concepts is influenced by national governments' and international organisations' food processing, trade, and regulatory policies as well as pedological and climatic factors and the level of agricultural technology development. To protect food producers and aid consumers in their purchasing decisions, the European Union (EU) encourages the use of various food quality schemes, including "Traditional Specialty Guaranteed" (TSG), "Protected Geographical Indication" (PGI), and "Protected Designation of Origin" (PDO). This review looks at previous research on how these labels affect consumer behaviour. 32 studies in all were discovered and organised. The international labels are more important in modern society and the pandemic circumstances brought on by COVID-19, thus even if these articles emphasise quite a variety of results, quality schemes are still useful in consumer decision- making processes.

Muca et al., (2022)4 Assess and evaluate consumer knowledge and preferences for local goods in three countries: Albania, Bulgaria, and Poland. (1) Historical context: The study focused on customer choices when provided with local items, especially awareness of their environmental friendliness. The research was motivated by the need to identify and assess changes in consumer behaviour as a consequence of the pandemic, as well as the worldwide difficulties associated with climate change and the broad need for environmental preservation. (2) Techniques: An online poll was done with 300 Poles, 262 Albanians, and 250 Bulgarians participating. A statistical analysis was used. (3) Findings: The study addressed research questions concerning customer willingness to pay a premium price and understanding of the effect of regional goods on the environment and rural residents' livelihoods. (4) Conclusions: The research demonstrated that a number of variables and driving forces impact consumer attitudes and behaviour in the three nations studied, depending on socioeconomic features and applicable legislation. COVID-19 enhanced the demand for items developed from environmentally friendly manufacturing techniques. Geographically indicated goods (GI products) are a preferable option in terms of sustainable consumption.

Goudis & Skuras, (2021)5 The objective of this study is to establish a categorization of European customers in terms of logo awareness, using demographic and socio-economic variables, and to examine the relationship between PDO awareness and consumer buying behaviour. The study used publicly accessible pan-European information obtained from Eurobarometer, which were acquired via four consecutive polls conducted between 2012 and 2017. The statistical analysis leverages the inherent spatial nesting structure of the data. The results of the study indicate the customer who is conscious of logos exhibits notable differences as compared to the typical European consumer. The statement elucidates the many categories of conscious and unconscious customers, prompting a discourse on strategies and techniques for engaging with the European consumer base. This research has a comprehensive pan-European viewpoint and encompasses several aspects such as customers' traits, behaviours, attitudes, as well as national and regional influences.

Radhika & Raju, (2021)6 Geographical Indications (GIs) demonstrate the need of include a quality assurance provision within the legislative framework of GIs if the advantages of registration are to flow to the agricultural community. A robust institutional backdrop and a well-organized supply chain may kickstart the potential beneficial effect of GI for stakeholders. Governmental assistance is required in this respect to develop successful promotional tactics to promote the product and its fundamental attributes across markets. The research examines the performance of rice GIs in Kerala, efforts implemented after registration, the gaps between planned and realised results of policy initiatives, and impediments in the implementation of innovation. The research reviewed suggest that the rebirth of the producer society is necessary in order to make collective choices on setting production limitations, deciding on a code of conduct, identifying quality indicators, and developing marketing and consumer orientation tactics.

Mishra, (2021)7 Discovered that the post-COVID economic crisis has resulted in huge unemployment and labour migration back to their homeland. These retrenched impoverished employees might utilise their traditional expertise to sustain their family while also creating local job prospects. Indian Geographical Indications legislation would be beneficial in safeguarding and marketing such indigenous items. This may be supplemented by India ratifying the Geneva Act to the Lisbon Agreement, which will go into effect in February 2020 and provides for a single-window registration of Geographical Indications in numerous countries. This article also exposes the gaps in Indian GI legislation that must be rectified in order to achieve the goal of the law. Finally, it is stated that the government should take necessary efforts to promote geographical indicators as a policy tool to aid the rural economy during these tough times.

Radhika et al., (2021)8 Geographical indication (GI) is a collective right, and its success is primarily dependent on the target groups' collective effort and good administration by the implementing agency. Using the Institutional Analysis and Development framework, the current research exposes the deficiencies in the institutional, technical, and participative components of GIs in the Indian setting. The rice GIs of Kerala chosen for the research are Navara Rice, Palakkadan Matta Rice, Pokkali Rice, Wayanad Jeerakasala Rice, Wayanad Gandhakasala Rice, and Kaipad Rice. The goal of GI designation was met in terms of protection, but since the registered owners did not undertake a participatory process in terms of marketing and promotion, no results were obtained save for Kaipad rice. Following GI registration, the average price of all rice GIs in Kerala rose. However, the issue is whether the price was high enough to maintain the growing of these speciality rices. These items are sold at a premium price to end users, yet the advantages do not reach the maker. The potential effects have been obscured by a lack of focused responses from institutional settings after GI identification.

Vandecandelaere et al., (2021)9 This study offers original research for developing a framework and database for the selection and application of appropriate sustainability indicators for geographic information systems (GIs). Several SSGI principles guided the work during an iterative process of reviewing, selecting, and improving relevant indicators, while the Sustainability Assessment of Food and Agriculture (SAFA) provided the structure to align with the Sustainable Development Goals (SDGs) and other widely used and recognised sustainability frameworks. As a consequence of this effort, a database of 372 rigorous sustainability indicators relevant to GIs has been created to aid practitioners in their usage. The debate emphasises the significance of the place-based approach and the participatory, inclusive process as the key to empowerment and the capacity to form coalitions. It also emphasises action and the need of improving both internal and external communication.

Pamukçu et al., (2021)10 With the advancement of technology, several tourist trends have emerged. Gastronomy tourism is one among them. For supply determinants to be effective in marketing efforts, it is vital to identify the elements that influence the growth of this form of tourism. One of these aspects is products registered with a geographical indicator. The study's goal in this regard is to investigate the impact of local cuisine and local goods with geographical indicators on the growth of gourmet tourism. Bolu, one of Turkey's cities, was chosen as the implementation site. The statistical package programme was used to solve the data. According to the study findings, local goods registered with geographical indications have the greatest influence on the growth of gastronomic tourism, with a 60% impact rate. The impact of regional foods with geographical identification is 37.7%.

Patel & Zala, (2021)11 In India, Geographical Indication (GI) has emerged as an important form of Intellectual Property Rights concern. It grants the right to utilise the product's indication to its makers or producers in that area. It also implies that they have the legal authority to restrict the use of any sign or name that does not have the features and characteristics guaranteed by the GI of that specific product. 370 goods were registered under GI in India through the 30th of September, 2020, out of 706 applications. Foreign nations have also registered certain items in India. For GI, 15 goods from 9 countries were registered. The current article focuses on the procedure of GI registration in India, the registration status of various goods by state and year, and the global picture of GI in force till 2018.

Di Vita et al., (2021)12 Geographical indications (PGI) for extra virgin olive oil (EVOO) were created in Italy to address the significant failure of protected designations of origin (PDO). This research seeks to uncover the traits customers anticipate in order to forecast market success. Design/methodology/approach: A survey was utilised in this research on a sample of consumers from Sicily, one of the first locations to produce a regional PGI for EVOO. Findings: The findings revealed that customers would accept this new product, and their expectations relate to a product with features such as green colour, not filtered, not sweet in flavour, and a well-known brand. Young guys might constitute a potential target. Practical implications: The findings predict whether this product will be approved and give direct suggestions for manufacturers interested in entering the market with a PGI EVOO. Originality/value: This investigation focuses on customer behaviour towards items that are expressly certified with a newly established PGI label, which are yet not widely available on the market.

Dos Reis Lopes et al., (2021)13 The conservation of geographical indications and the application of PDO, PGI, or TSG quality labels for high-quality regional agri-food products is a factor that stimulates growth in European regions by enhancing the endogenous potential of their territory. As such, the current study attempts to comprehend the existing link between these items and tourist demand in their native areas via an examination of consumer behaviour. The approach employed to reach this goal included an online and in-person survey of agri-food product customers in Spain and Portugal, as well as a thorough evaluation of secondary sources. The findings indicate that customers are generally aware of quality marks or seals and their significance. It also proved the presence of a significant symbiotic relationship between these items and tourism in their original countries, owing to their tremendous capacity to mobilise their customers.

Rabadán et al., (2021)14 examine the significance of the geographical indication (GI) label in the marketing of lamb meat in comparison to other major qualities. Our results support the strong relationship that consumers have in their thoughts between the provenance of lamb meat and the protected geographical indicator (PGI). Nonetheless, it is worth mentioning that the consumer categories identified in this study place a higher value on several qualities of PGI lamb meat, which may be connected to socioeconomic variables. In this regard, fewer ethnocentric customers with a higher wealth and education level have a preference for the breed of lamb, but more ethnocentric consumers have a preference for brand name. Due to the existing overlap between the demand for PGI goods and other features, consumers may view a product lacking PGI but featuring particular reference to all of those attributes similarly. The PGI label may help to decrease search efforts and delays in this respect.

Chakrabarti, (2021)15 Geographical indicators have been of significant importance in safeguarding handicrafts, as well as agricultural and industrial products, within the context of India. A considerable number of products have already been officially recognised as geographical indications, with a significant number of other products now through the registration process. This paper conducts an analysis of the registered items so far and identifies specific concerns associated with the Indian Geographical Indication (GI) protection. It proposes many potential ways to address these difficulties.

U Priyanka, (2021)16 GI tagged products includes agricultural and handcrafted items that have been recognised under the Geographical Indication Act of 1999. Kerala has 28 Gi-tagged items, giving it enormous potential. Shimp and Sharma introduced the noble notion of regional ethnocentrism in 1987. To quantify ethnocentrism, a 17-point "CETSCALE" was devised, and it is widely used in marketing literature. This study underlines the effect of regional ethnocentrism on the purchasing of Geographically Indicated (GI) labelled items by highlighting the research gap. The regional ethnocentrism regarding GI Tagged items was investigated. Based on the results, manufacturers were given very helpful advice on how to successfully promote regional geographically specified items. Regional ethnocentrism may be embraced as an attractive and successful approach, allowing smaller producers to thrive in this technologically globalised world.

Sgroi, (2021)17 Geographical indicators (GIs) are increasingly being seen as a tool for promoting long-term local development. The research focuses on how geographical indicators might contribute to a territorial public system and how this can be jeopardised by a number of market failures. Using economic literature on public goods as a foundation, this article demonstrates how geographical indicators, and their legal protection, may provide a sustainable growth model. The paper tries to show and create fresh economic reasons in favour of a more comprehensive political approach to Geographical Indications' contribution to sustainable development. The study's findings emphasise how territorial public goods based on cohesiveness serve as a vector for the resilience of the agricultural landscape and the development of the whole area in which the agri-food product is created. The importance of product and area information is a crucial feature, as proven in the article. Dominance at the competitive system level and societal cohesiveness no longer guarantee agri-food production success. The research demonstrates that the effectiveness of GIs is dependent on the function of communication in conveying information.

Duvaleix et al., (2021)18 Geographical indications protection is increasingly an essential part of trade agreements. This study looked at whether geographical indicators are appreciated by international customers and if they have consequences for firm-level commerce. Using French Customs firm-product level data and a unique dataset of businesses and products affected by Protected Designations of Origin (PDO) in the cheese and butter industry. The results suggest that consumers consider PDO varieties to be of greater quality than non-PDO varieties, and that PDO prices are 11.5% higher than non-PDO pricing. Firms producing PDO varieties do not export more, but they do profit from easier access to European markets and nations with comparable geographical indication policies. The inclusion of select GI types in trade treaties may therefore provide a chance for PDO growers to expand their market access.

Fernández-Zarza et al., (2021)19 digs into the aspects on which the perception of quality of a product is constructed. Two localised agri-food systems (LAS), one for Iberian acorn-ham from Spain and the other for chorizo from Toluca in Mexico. A study of those food systems in two distinct socio-political situations was undertaken using a hybrid methodology that used quantitative and qualitative methodologies. This technique recognised the significance of informal instruments, which are based not just on institutionalised certification but also on informal processes such as trust and closeness between producers and customers. The findings of this research demonstrate how food quality categories may be directed by different logics based on the setting, categories, and types of stakeholders involved. The study proposes a food quality categorization based on the trust conceptual framework. This categorization enables GIs valorisation efforts to see the aspects on which they may be led to work with the various attributes in their LAS.

Menggala et al., (2021)20 focuses on the value chain effect of Koerintji cinnamon geographical indications (GIs). The research was carried out at Talang Kemuning, Kerinci regency, Indonesia, from September to November 2017. To determine if GIs enhance revenue, source of production, and product quality, a village farmers' group was studied using a semi-structured questionnaire, roundtable discussions, interviews, and direct observations. The literature on the issue was analysed using a descriptive technique, and a value chain study was constructed based on the review's results. This assisted us in better understanding how the impacts of GIs are distributed across chain players and finally reach the places where GI goods originate. GIs bring value, particularly for farmers and purchasers. Farmers and purchasers' efficiency has increased by adopting the GI Koerintji cinnamon's handbook of criteria. According to the findings, producers created a method to monitor post-harvest processing in order to ensure a safe and high-quality supply to the global spice market. TAKTIK members undertake specified processes, such as choosing raw materials, grading, origin verification, and quality control, in accordance with the book criteria. GIs also allow farmers to claim a price premium. As a consequence, the existence of GI Koerintji cinnamon has increased the value and trustworthiness of TAKTIK farmers, resulting in price increases.

Hoang et al., (2020)21 Explores the link between geographical indications (GIs) and sustainable rural development in Vietnam, using the Cao Phong orange as a case study. Interviews with Vietnamese policymakers and orange growers yielded qualitative data on the role of the Vietnamese government in designing and implementing GIs, as well as the involvement of local producers who benefit from GIs, in order to determine how and to what extent GI protection affects sustainable rural development. The findings indicate that GIs have favourably contributed to long-term rural development in Vietnam; nonetheless, certain issues persist. The paper closes with policy recommendations for boosting GIs and long-term rural development in Vietnam.

Lee et al., (2020)22 Using a non-hypothetical experimental auction in the field, researchers studied consumers' valuations of geographical indication (GI) and protected geographical indication (PGI)-labeled rice in Bangkok. We also investigated the impact of giving regional indicator information sequentially on product value. According to the findings, customers are prepared to pay a premium for rice with geographical certificates, with the biggest premium being paid for rice with both GI and PGI certifications. The availability of specific information regarding geographical indicators raises the premiums even further. Consumers, on the other hand, incur a welfare loss as a result of the existing high market pricing for rice with regional certificates. To get customer benefit from the establishment of GI and PGI certification, a price reduction of around 10% would be required.

Quiñones-Ruiz et al., (2020)23 Explained how the necessity for collective action expressed itself in four coffee PGIs in Colombia, Indonesia, and Thailand. examined the cases using a common analytical approach based on Elinor Ostrom's Institutional Analysis and Development (IAD) framework, which includes: i) the contextual setting of the product and territory; ii) the actors involved; iii) institutional arrangements and action arena; and

iv) the outcome of these arrangements. A producer organisation (Colombia), a social foundation and a commercial corporation (Thailand), and a government-supported consortium (Indonesia) were among the petitioners in the cases. The process of institutionalising the GI requires strong and well-resourced players to take the lead, with minimal input from genuine producers. As a result, such compliance with the EU criterion for collective action was mostly regarded as an administrative formality, rather than actually satisfying the IAD standards for successful collective action. The design of collective action processes' guiding principles is thought to have a substantial impact on their success and the distribution of any benefits gained. This article focuses on how the positionality and specific interests of the actors involved shape this design, as well as their varying power and influence, diverse attitudes towards moral legitimacy, and varying relationships with external actors such as development agents, research organisations, and state agencies.

Bashir., (2020)24 Geographical Indication protection is becoming an increasingly critical problem for producers who see improved legal protection for their product at the national and international levels as one of their primary issues. The goal of this essay is to examine and critique the flaws in India's GI protection system, including challenges in protecting and enforcing GI rights. The paper goes on to analyse data from a survey conducted by the researcher on GIs in India and interactions with stakeholders. An examination of the legislative framework, statistics on GIs in India, and interactions with stakeholders reveal that the legal framework available for GI protection is relatively limited in terms of breadth, impact, and protection. The sale of counterfeit items results in a loss of income for the manufacturers. To reinforce the present GI protection system, there is a need to raise awareness regarding the protection of geographical indication goods across India. Although national law has created the path for the protection of geographical indications, the government expects producers and stakeholders to recognise their duties and register their goods under the GI Act.

Marie-Vivien, (2020)25 Investigates how GIs have evolved in ASEAN and Asia, the world's most active new market for GIs. We investigate the various laws and their actual application in eight of the ten ASEAN nations with a sui generis system (Vietnam, Cambodia, Thailand, Indonesia, Malaysia, Laos, Singapore, and Myanmar), as well as India and Japan, two Asian countries with active GI policies. Based on a comparative analysis of these countries and EU GI regulations, this paper focuses on the following aspects of the GI system: the sui generis institutional system and the types of goods protected by GIs, the scope of protection against misuses, the nature of applicants, and the nature of GI control before and after registration. The report then discusses convergences and similar difficulties, as well as possible ideas for GI success in Asia. The biggest obstacles that Asian nations face are the many registered GIs that are not being utilised on the market i.e. they are Sleeping Beauties waiting to be woken. This is explained by ASEAN and Asian nations' convergence on a top-down state-driven strategy. Moving ahead, we advocate increased participation of collective organisations in bringing together value chain stakeholders who should play a fundamental role in developing and maintaining GIs.

Youkta-Kumari., (2020)26 Geographical Indications have gained prominence as a crucial property rights problem in a nation like India, where there is tremendous variety on cultural and geographical grounds, and which, if used intelligently, may benefit the country greatly. However, there are various obstacles and concerns that are causing certain Indian states to fall behind while others are functioning well. The goal of this research is to discover the causes for the discrepancy in GI registration across states. The research uses secondary sources such as WIPO, WTO, Manupatra.com, IPI, case studies from literatures, journals, books, and so on, and explains it using bar graphs and pie charts. The study's results will have substantial consequences for both the Central and State Governments of India in terms of tackling this difficulty and establishing strategies to maximise the potential advantages of Geographical Indications.

Chinthaginjala et al., (2020)27 Geographical Indications (GIs) are a primary intellectual resource about a variety of goods, as well as a tool for protecting consumer welfare and strengthening assurance in high-quality and local products, as well as a legal and financial tool for rural expansion and cultural heritage protection. Since India's admission to the WTO (World Trade Organisation) in 1995, intellectual property law has been a hotly disputed subject. As a result, the geography, quality, and renown of the product are distinct from anything else. This enables the manufacturer to communicate the accomplishments of their goods to customers in the declaration of information lack of equality.

D'souza & Joshi, (2019)28 Udupi jasmine farming contributes significantly to the economic and social development of the jasmine growing community-based industry in coastal Karnataka, India. It aids in the promotion of rural livelihoods, food security, and poverty alleviation. Because of the considerable socioeconomic effect of jasmine growing, jasmine promotion and marketing are unavoidable for the survival of this community-based industry. The purpose of this research is to create an e-commerce platform for strategic marketing and promotion of Udupi jasmine. According to the findings, the advantages of e-business are not being used in the current system. Because Udupi jasmine is a one-of-a-kind crop with a geographical indication tag (GI), it cannot be grown under normal agricultural conditions. The study is to advocate the use of a customised e-commerce framework for jasmine in light of the present crude system. This will strengthen the socioeconomic development of this community-based company since agricultural goods will be circulated on a greater scale.

Pushpa Gowri (2019)29 comprehensive analysis of the literature on diverse studies connected to brand image and consumer purchase decisions, which investigates the many elements of brand image and their effect on customer purchasing decisions According to the study, brand image is the soul of the brand. It is the customer's perception of the brand's overall personality. The author concludes that brands help customers make more informed purchasing decisions. When consumers are aware of brands that meet their demands, they make swift purchasing decisions. People pick products that complement their lifestyle and improve their quality of life.

Divya, N D Anoop, K K., (2018)30 in most developed and emerging nations, digitalization has become the norm. Digitalization refers to the process of transforming data into a digital representation. The globe has evolved into a digital village. Digital marketing is a marketing sector experiment. Aranmula Kannadi is a product with a Geographical Indication. It's a handmade metal combination mirror produced in Aranmula, a tiny residential hamlet in the state of Kerala. The study's goal was to examine the impact of digitalization on Aranmula Kannadi sales. The research was carried out on thirty Aranmula Kannadi manufacturers. The information was gathered by delivering questionnaires to the chosen producers. The demographics were analysed using descriptive statistics, and the study goals were analysed using the 't' test. The study's findings revealed that digitalization greatly boosts Aranmula Kannadi sales.

Babu s, Kumaran.N., (2018) 31 The Indian E-commerce business industry is vastly underutilised. Manufacturers of GI Tagged items may capitalise on this potential if they raise consumer knowledge about the GI Tagged products and their availability online. The goal of this research is to raise consumer awareness of GI-tagged items by gauging their readiness to purchase them online. 24 GI tagged items from Tamilnadu were taken, and the degree of awareness of these products was examined using 150 samples gathered from Madurai, Virudhunagar, and Sivakasi using structured questionnaire. To establish their amount of effect on the purchase of GI labelled items, criteria such as quality, price, pride, emotional connection, and recollection of site of visit were investigated. People like GI-tagged things mostly because they have an emotional relationship to the product.

Neilson et al., (2018) 32 The ideas of value capture and strategic coupling from the Global Production Networks (GPN) literature are used in this research to examine the developmental consequences of officially registered (protected) GIs in the Indonesian coffee industry. Based on an analysis of variables along a logical effect route, our research reveals minimal evidence and a low chance of concrete economic gains for coffee producers in Indonesia as a consequence of existing GIs, at least in the near future. This low developmental performance is explained by the failure of local institutional frameworks enabling GIs to strategically pair with the actor practises of leading coffee corporations. However, the GIs seem to provide certain stakeholders with intangible advantages in terms of developing a feeling of regional pride and cultural identity. While one objective of GIs is to make a moral claim over the geographical and cultural property represented in consumer items, achieving rural development results requires significantly deeper interaction with extra-legal moral principles along the value chain.

Verma & Mishra, (2018) 33 Examines the identification and marketing prospects of 'Banaras Brocades and Sarees', a handloom product that was granted a Geographical Indication (GI) tag in 2009. This research examines the prevailing industry trends and market factors that influence the handloom product sector, specifically focusing on Banarsi Sarees. Despite the adoption of steps aimed at safeguarding the integrity of weaving as an art form, the granting of Geographical Indication (GI) designation being a significant milestone in this endeavour, there is a dearth of strategic planning and effective execution of post-GI measures necessary to fully capitalise on its economic viability. The research proposes tactics for brand creation and marketing of 'Banaras Brocades and Sarees' in both Indian and foreign markets, with the aim of capitalising on the commercial advantages associated with the 'GI' tag.

Tashiro et al., (2018)34 Sheds information on (1) phase-by-phase internal mechanisms of GI registration and (2) connections between application length and perceived effects of GI registration in Northwestern Japan. In Japan,

GI is a relatively new system that was implemented in 2015. The criteria for analysing the gap in GI registration effects among the seven GI instances were descriptive and analytical, including information and data derived from official papers, a questionnaire survey, and personal conversations with GI applicants' key informants. To visualise the complicated internal GI registration processes and their impacts, qualitative information was combined with quantitative data. This study showed that GI applicants who spent a long time to complete GI registration tended to perceive relatively mild registration effects. GI applicants who took a very short time to complete their GI registration, on the other hand, tended to rate the registration favourably. The most challenging aspects of the application preparation procedure were preparing the application documentation and long-term engagement with a GI regulator. Conclusion: This study discusses ways for uncovering the complicated, both ex-ante and ex-post, GI registration procedures in order to reorganise present members of GI applicants, fill gaps, and improve the impacts of GI registration.

Bernabéu et al., (2018)35 Factors that influence customers' preferences in the purchase of lamb meat is a crucial element in enhancing the market demand for this particular product. In order to achieve this objective, Researcher used conjoint analysis to ascertain the preferences of lamb meat customers based on their consumption frequency. Additionally, utilised logistic simulation to examine the market shares of the traits that were deemed most valuable. Based on our market segmentation analysis, it appears that habitual and occasional consumers of lamb meat exhibit distinct preferences. Regular consumers primarily prioritise the origin of the meat, whereas occasional consumers consider additional attributes such as Protected Geographical Origin (PGI) and organic production. A comprehensive examination of market shares reveals that PGI has a substantial influence on consumer choices, while ecological production exhibits a comparatively less pronounced effect. This discovery validates the efficacy of PGI (Protected Geographical Indication) in the lamb meat industry and underscores the pressing need to enhance the communication strategy of the organic agriculture sector as a means of synergistically augmenting its consumer acceptability.

Babu and Kumar, (2018) 36 The research study on Exploring customers' awareness about Geographical Indication Tagged Products and their willingness to purchase it through online. The study identified the awareness of GI products among customers. One fifty samples were used to collect data. Twenty-Four GI Tagged Products of Tamil Nadu were only considered for the study. The results indicated a low awareness of GI Tagged Products, which affected the readiness to buy the product online. People preferred the product mainly due to the emotional attachment and remembrance of the place of visit.

Pushpa Gowri and Anitha Ramachander (2018) 37 in the author clearly point that kancheepuram is a silk paradise of south India the author state the uniqueness of kancheepuram saree, where three single threads of mulberry silk yarn is twisted with jari to produce a saree which is not found in any other saree. The designs are taken from sculptures of temples. The researcher states, in kancheepuram there are around 60,000 silk weavers in the city, 50,000 weavers work under co-operative fold. Finally the researcher conclude, wearing a kancheepuram saree at festivals and rituals is considered auspicious. Despite the transition from traditional handloom to contemporary power loom, the sector has kept its viewpoint by pleasing modern clients.

Thangaraja and Abirami, (2018)38 The research study on the Consumer Experience on Geographical Indicators and its Impact on Purchase Decision: An Empirical Study. The study determined consumers' experience on GI tagged products and their impact on purchase decisions. The sample consists of 224 customers. The study covers the areas of Kochi. SEM model was developed to analyse the impact of customer experience on the purchase decision Price, brand, location, advertising, labelling, supply chain, service mix, and atmosphere were identified as factors to analyse customer experience. Brand familiarity, product differentiation, hedonic price, word of mouth experience on the variable GI. The model results indicate that customer experience positively impacts purchase decisions and GI favourably influences.

Vinayan., (2017) 39 Since India's accession to the World Trade Organisation in 1995, the intellectual property regime has been a hotly disputed matter. This has resulted in the creation of new laws, such as the Geographical Indications Act of 1999 (GI Act) and the Plant Varieties Protection Act of 2001, as well as the revision of previous intellectual property laws in India, such as the Patents Act of 1970. Geographical Indications (GIs) are used to designate items as coming from a certain place as a quality indicator. As a result, the geography, quality, and reputation of the product are all closely intertwined. In the context of information asymmetry, this allows the manufacturer to express the credentials of their items to customers. This paper examines the legal framework in India for the protection of origin labelled goods as Geographical Indications, as well as the policy difficulties and controversies surrounding the usage and registration of GIs under the Geographical Indications of Goods (Registration and Protection) Act 1999.

Yang et al., (2017)40 There are more and more reasons for American consumers to acquire and consume local food items. One emphasises the significance of the origin of the things they buy. A second, and related, cause is worry about food miles, or the distance foods have travelled from where they are produced or farmed to where they are bought or eaten. While "eating local" is often described as advantageous and virtuous (for example, health, environment, community development, and civic duty), it also entails challenges such as the time and sometimes skills necessary for both buying and preparation. Such restrictions often dissuade many people from purchasing local fresh vegetables. This article is based on the findings of many focus groups with Michigan customers who are devoted to eating locally. The study provides insights into how these consumers deal with or balance their commitment to eating locally with the restrictions they confront while purchasing and cooking locally grown food.

Dewi et al., (2017)41 Consumer behaviour was investigated at all stages of the purchasing decision process to identify their impression of agro-geographical indication goods and the most important qualities in the purchasing choice process of the products. The necessity of product authenticity was discovered at the first stage of the purchasing decision process; the internet and social media as the major source of GI's product knowledge was discovered at the second stage; and product indigenousness was discovered at the third level. At the fourth stage, the majority of customers purchased the product in the conventional market; and at the fifth stage, we discovered that the majority of them were happy with the product, its price, and planned to buy more in the future. The majority of consumers have a favourable opinion of GI goods. They had not, however, prioritised GI items above other comparable products. The quality of the GI goods was the most important consideration in the purchasing choice.

Huibin Zhan et al., (2016)42 a model was developed to identify the characteristics impacting consumer loyalty to geographical indication goods. The study explores the elements that improve consumer loyalty and the extent to which these factors have an influence. According to the findings of the study, customers' views toward producing places, perceived quality, and knowledge of geographical indication protection are major variables influencing their loyalty to geographical indication products. This study is classified as exploratory research since it used the grey incidence analysis approach.

Raju & Tiwari, (2015)43 In order to comply with the Trade Related Aspects of Intellectual Property Rights (TRIPs) Agreement under the World Trade Organisation (WTO) Agreements, India approved the Geographical Indications of Goods (Registration & Protection) Act, 1999. Geographical indications are defined in Article 22 of the TRIPs Agreement as "the indications that identify a good as originating in the territory of a Member, or a region or locality within that territory, where a given quality, reputation, or other characteristic of the good is essentially attributable to its geographical origin." Many developing nations, including as India, have implemented laws to provide more and better protection for GI in order to improve the economic position of the impoverished people who contribute to many essential export items. The paper re-examines the issues that will face the Act's implementation and proposes further revisions to the Act to effectively preserve Indian indigenous knowledge and the reputation of items originating in India. It also tries to identify what else is needed to reap the benefits of registration, as well as problematic areas such as who is the right applicant for a GI application, Part-B registration of beneficiaries, marketing of GI products, maintaining product quality, counterfeiting, and enforcement mechanisms. It is stated that in the future, India would need a concerted effort by the Central and State Governments, GI owners, and beneficiaries to safeguard and develop Indian GIs.

William Van et al., (2014)44 currently, the EU is the major holder of protected GIs, and the EU claims that they are widely and successfully utilised as a rural and regional development instrument in EU nations. Until now, Australia's reaction to GIs has been mostly determined by views of their influence on trade gains and losses. Because of an agreement with the EU, Australia now only has legal protection for wine-related GI's. Given the increased international focus on GIs, particularly in China and India, we ask whether Australia should seriously consider a special regime for the legal protection of GIs in relation to agricultural products and foodstuffs in general, something that has not been investigated to date due to Australia's negative attitude towards GI protection in international trade negotiations. This study outlines the problems and potential associated with evaluating GI development in the context of Australia's regional, rural, and remote diversity.

Albayram et al., (2014)45 The research paper on investigated on Purchasing Local and Non – Local Products Labelled with Geographical Indications (GIs). The study determined the consumer behaviour towards labelled products with Geographical Indications. Locally and non-locally produced were identified for the study. Consumers' willingness to pay for both cases was estimated, and the frequency of buying the products was measured utilising 271 questionnaires. Factor analysis was run to show the main factors in accordance with consumers' behaviour. The results demonstrated that consumers behave reliably according to local GI labelled products. Primarily, the quality and origin of the products play significant roles in consumers' purchase decisions.

Rudawska., (2014)46 According to the study, over 90% of respondents had a favourable opinion of traditional items. The study's findings corroborate customers' favourable and emotional opinions towards conventional items. This emotional tie, which is critical in building customer loyalty, drives individuals to purchase traditional foods. Traditional items that are seen as fresh and natural by Polish customers are well received. Consumers greatly value the quality of traditional items and emphasise their beneficial impact on their and their families' health. According to the study, Polish customers pay little attention to geographical and quality signals, which are intended to create a trustworthy picture of the product. Traditional items are seen as pricey, making it harder to establish loyalty and influencing purchase frequency. Almost 40% of respondents purchase conventional items once a month.

Albayram et al., (2014)47 investigated customer attitudes towards product quality, specifically towards local and non-local items labelled with geographical indications (GIs). As a result, two GI goods were found, both locally and non-locally manufactured, for the same market (IZMIR) and with similar customer potentials. Furthermore, customer sentiments towards these two goods, one local (South Aegean Olive Oil) and one non-local (Ayvalik Olive Oil), were analysed and contrasted. The willingness to pay of consumers in both situations was calculated, and the frequency with which they purchased the items was measured. A factor analysis was performed to identify the most important elements influencing customer behaviour. Following that, these components were examined using binary logistic regression to determine the factors impacting customer attributes and to investigate factor interactions. The findings show that customers react consistently in response to locally GI-labeled items. Primarily, the quality and origin of the items influence customer purchasing choices, and people rely more on local products than non-local ones.

Anson and Pavithran., (2014)48 this study the author initially gave a said, geographical indication is useful in protecting the geographically linked products as well as against imitation the researcher tries to study the views among the pokkali rice (a protected geographical indication product) producers. The researcher find that organized marketing will bring more prosit, can reduce the entry of duplicates into the market and will promote business. The study is limited to specific product. Further research may try in another geographical indication product.

Dolli., (2012)49 Intellectual Property Rights (IPR) were fundamentally recognised and accepted all over the world for a variety of reasons, including providing incentives to individuals for new creations, providing due recognition to creators and inventors, ensuring monetary reward for intellectual property, and ensuring the availability of genuine and original products. Since India is one of the fastest rising countries with a diverse industrial base and a sustainable economic growth motto, it has prioritised research and development. Recognising the significance of innovations, India accepted the World Trade Organisation (WTO) accord. This agreement also underlines India's adherence to the Trade Related Aspects of Intellectual Property Rights (TRIPS). To demonstrate its legislative significance, the Ministry of Commerce and Industry established the Department of Industrial Policy and Promotion as the Government of India's main department for all issues relating Intellectual Property. In light of the above, this article examines the legislation and developments in intellectual property in India, including patents, designs, trademarks, and geographical indications.

Das., (2012)50 Geographical Indications (GIs) have recently surfaced as a key intellectual property rights concern in the Indian environment. Since the Indian GI Act went into effect on September 15, 2003, more than a hundred Indian items have been recognised as GIs. However, when it comes to realising the potential advantages embedded in GIs, stakeholders in India face a number of practical hurdles. Apart from effective enforcement of rights in relevant markets (domestic and export), the success of a GI is heavily reliant on appropriate marketing and promotion of the product - tasks that are not only resource-intensive but also difficult to execute for many stakeholders in a developing country like India. It is much more difficult to guarantee that a fair part of the advantages arising from a product's GI designation reaches the real producers/artisans downstream the supply chain unless a suitable institutional structure is in place. Against this context, the paper aims to investigate India's chances for capitalising on the potential advantages implicit in GIs, as well as the significant hurdles facing the nation in its efforts to realise such benefits.

Vinayan., (2012)51 Local, national, and global actors affect livelihood choices regardless of geographical context via their policies, institutional structure, and procedures. The implementation of intellectual property rights (IPR) under the WTO framework highlights how international choices influence millions of lives throughout the world. This has compelled national governments to establish new rules and regulations, such as India's Geographical Indications Act in 1999. The inclusion of Geographical Indications (GIs) under the World Trade Organization's Trade-Related Aspects of Intellectual Property Rights (TRIPS) Agreement has been praised by developing nations for its ability to encourage rural development, produce wealth, and safeguard traditional knowledge. The premium that customers are ready to pay for a GI certified product is intimately tied to the product's quality. This necessitates a complete reorganisation of the supply chain to guarantee not just quality but also that the income generated by GI is dispersed evenly across the supply chain. This demands the building of ties between stakeholders at all levels in order to promote confidence and ease market access. In this context, the article investigates the fundamental issues associated in the implementation of GIs, a crucial component of IPR, in traditional livelihood sectors such as handloom weaving in India, relying on global success stories of GIs.

Ali., (2011)52 Geographical indications (GIs) have grown in relevance in terms of legal development and economic diplomacy since their inclusion in the World Trade Organization's Trade-Related Intellectual Property Agreement (TRIPS). Its significance for older economies and nations with a strong agricultural basis has grown exponentially. In this article, I examined the application of TRIPS Agreement GI provisions in Pakistan, where agricultural accounts for a significant portion of the country's Gross Domestic Product (GDP). Despite the fact that Pakistan, like India, has hundreds of GIs, there is not a single registration of GIs under the current legal framework. As a result, gaps in the legal framework for GIs in Pakistan are investigated. Comparable instances include the establishment of the Sui Generis Law of GIs in India and the GI Regulations of the European Union (EU). I also examined the potential of GIs in Pakistan, as well as the economic component of GIs in terms of its relationship to development. Finally, examined the obstacles, the role of the state, and the path ahead.

Seetisarn & Chiaravutthi., (2011)53 The research study on Thai Consumer's Willingness to Pay for Food Products with Geographical Indications. The study investigated the Thai Consumers' Willingness to Pay (WTP) for products with GI labels. This experiment was carried out under the nth price auction method on Doi Tung Coffee, Tung Kula Ronghai Thai Hom Mali rice, and Chaiya salted eggs. Sixty participants were asked to offer bids for three products each with different types of labels, a normal label; a label stating the product's origin; and a label which stated the product's origin and contained a GI sign. The results showed that the product's origin influences Thai consumers' WTPs. However, the WTPs of GI labels do not significantly differ from the WTPs of labels which state the product's origin.

Adinolfi et al., (2011)54 look into public perception of regional wines having designations of origin. According to the findings, a designation of origin is a required but not sufficient criterion for effective market performance. Limitations/implications of the research: Implications for marketing tactics are obvious: wine production is distinguished by many realms of production, and marketing methods should be significant. Originality/value: The passion for designations of origin is not always justified: the abundance of designations of origin may desensitise consumers, having serious consequences for rural areas whose livelihood revolves upon the production of high-quality wines. In order to get an appellation, organisational changes and more effective communication techniques are required.

Kulkarni & Konde., (2011)55 Geographical Indications (GIs) have recently arisen as an important type of intellectual property rights in the Indian environment. Given the financial potential of handicrafts, proper legal protection of GIs is required to prevent their unauthorised use. The unlawful use of geographical names not only harms the reputation of the original product, but also deprives real right holders of returns on investments for creating products and their market reputation. Furthermore, people are likely to be duped into buying counterfeits. This document presents a review of the current situation of registered GIs, their categorization in terms of handicrafts, and their registrations by location. More significantly, this article emphasises the need of improving current pre- and post-registration GI procedures, as well as its reinforcing methods, as crucial variables in the development of India's handicrafts business.

Piemkhoontham and Ruenrom., (2010)56 Found that Thai customers were prepared to pay a premium for meat with traceability marks that indicated safe to eat quality. However, a consumer's pre-purchase decision-making and the criteria he may consider in selecting a quality product remain unknown and need more analysis. Many research have focused on the demographic factors that influence the buying intention of GI-labeled items. Few research have focused on creating causal models on customer response to GI labels while purchasing indigenous items. The current research seeks to address this void by investigating the impact of product diagnosticity supplied by the GI label on perceived quality, which leads to customer trust and purchase intention. By conducting a survey among domestic Indian handloom clothes customers, the study hopes to contribute to the traditional handloom apparel marketing industry.

Das., (2010)57 Geographical indications (GIs) have arisen as a major intellectual property rights concern in India. Since the Indian GI Act went into effect on September 15, 2003, more than a hundred Indian items have been recognised as GIs. However, when it comes to realising the potential advantages embedded in GIs, stakeholders in India face a number of practical hurdles. Aside from effective enforcement of rights in relevant markets (domestic and export), the success of a GI is heavily reliant on appropriate marketing and promotion of the product—tasks that are not only resource-intensive but also difficult to execute for many stakeholders in a developing country like India. It is much more difficult to guarantee that a fair part of the advantages arising from a product's GI status reaches the real producers/artisans downstream in the supply chain unless an adequate institutional framework is in place. Against this context, the paper aims to investigate India's chances for capitalising on the potential advantages contained in GIs, as well as the significant hurdles facing the nation in its efforts to realise such benefits.

Bramley et al., (2009)58 The study's goal is to learn about customers' perceptions of GI labels, which serve as a decision-making tool in the traditional handloom garment consumer setting. This is important in the traditional handloom garment market, because it is difficult to tell the difference between fabric made on a hand-operated loom and cloth made on a mechanised loom. Chendamangalam Handlooms, Kuthampulli Handlooms, Kasaragod Sarees, and Balaramapuram Handlooms in Kerala, India, have been authorised to carry the GI designation by the GI registry. GI has been created to aid with the verification of items having a place of origin and indigenous practices/traits. This also serves as legal protection, since the GI label assumes the existence of a reputation.

Fragata et al., (2007)59 The position in Portugal in terms of state policies and the market for agrifood products with Protected Designation of Origin (PDO) and Protected Geographical Indication (PGI) under Council Regulation is reported. Based on the Portuguese experience, several new issues in the institutional framework of the protection system and policies related to rural development are described. Significant disparities in distribution networks are noted between product categories and among items within the same sector. The development of Portuguese PDO/PGI goods will vary greatly depending on the product and industry. This development will be influenced by both the dynamics and the capabilities of supply networks to export higher-quality goods. The majority of Portuguese customers are unaware with the notion of PDO or PGI. However, the conduct of a major portion of customers indicates that the geographical origin and reputations of regions are essential in consumer impressions. There seems to be a substantial positive link between the choice for PDO/PGI goods and various major socioeconomic indicators such as education level, buying capacity, social class, and kind of occupation/profession among Portuguese consumers.

Das., (2006)60 Geographical indications (GIs) protection has emerged as one of the most controversial intellectual property rights problems in the World Trade Organisation (WTO). With its near-universal scope and enforcement, the Trade-Related Aspects of Intellectual Property Rights (TRIPS) Agreement has the potential to offer adequate protection for all GIs. Even with TRIPS in place, the current status of international protection for all GIs, except those designating wines and spirits, is far from adequate because TRIPS mandates a two-level system of protection for GIs: (i) basic protection applicable to all GIs (under Article 22) and additional protection for GIs designating wines and spirits (under Article 23). India, along with other like-minded nations, has long fought at the WTO to broaden the scope of Article 23 protection to include all goods. The current article addresses this contentious subject, which has now at a virtual standstill.

Skuras & Vakrou., (2002)61 Quality agricultural goods are playing an increasingly significant role in the agricultural and food policy of the European Union (EU). The potential for distinguishing quality goods and services on a regional basis has been identified, and legislation to preserve geographical indications and designations of origin for agricultural products and high-quality foodstuffs has been adopted. Today, marketing tactics for high- quality goods seek to capitalise on these new prospects by leveraging the products' reputation and the image of their place of origin. A dichotomous choice model is used in this research to discover the socioeconomic aspects that impact Greek customers' willingness to pay for an origin branded wine. According to the findings, wine buyers' willingness to pay changes solely according to socioeconomic and demographic factors. In addition, the mean willingness to pay was calculated using two different econometric assumptions of the dichotomous choice model. We discovered that non-quality wine buyers are prepared to spend double the price of a bottle of regular table wine provided the alternative includes a guarantee of the wine's provenance. Their judgement is discovered to be solely based on education and affinity with the place of origin. The model parameters are compared, and important conclusions about pricing and marketing of origin-labeled wines are derived.

RESEARCH GAP

Despite the increasing prevalence and international acknowledgement of geographical indication (GI) products, there exists a substantial knowledge gap regarding consumer behaviour towards these distinctive goods that are tied to specific locations. Numerous scholarly investigations have delved into diverse facets concerning Geographical Indication (GI) products and their ramifications on regional economies and producers. However, there exists a dearth of comprehensive research on the precise determinants that shape consumer decision-making and preferences towards GI products. The identified research gap holds significant importance and justifies the need for additional investigation. This is necessary in order to improve the marketing and promotion strategies for Geographical Indication (GI) products, thereby ensuring their long-term development and competitiveness within the market By addressing these research gaps, valuable contributions can be made to the existing academic literature on consumer behaviour and geographical indications. Furthermore, this research has the potential to offer practical implications for producers, policymakers, and marketers. Specifically, it can aid in the development of effective strategies that enhance the recognition, demand, and competitiveness of geographically indicated products in the global market.

CHAPTER III

THEORETICAL FRAME WORK

GEOGRAPHICAL INDICATION

In contemporary society, Intellectual Property has assumed a prominent role in both the economic and social spheres. Intellectual property encompasses the tangible and intangible creations of the human intellect. Intellectual property laws aim to protect the interests of creators by granting them limited rights to control the use of their intellectual assets. The recognition of the importance of intellectual property rights was initially realised through the establishment of the Paris Convention for the Protection of Industrial Property in 1883 and the Berne Convention for the Protection of Literary and Artistic Works in 1886. Both settlements are under the jurisdiction of the World Intellectual Property Organisation (WIPO). Intellectual Property Rights can be classified into two distinct classifications, namely industrial property rights and copyright, based on the scope of application and the nature of utilisation. Industrial property rights refer to the legal protection granted to businesses and trade in relation to their tangible and intangible assets. These rights encompass the examination and safeguarding of various aspects that are deemed beneficial for enterprises and commercial activities. Industrial Property encompasses various forms of intellectual property rights, such as patents for inventions, trademarks, industrial designs, and geographical indications. Therefore, the intellectual property framework serves to establish a balance between the interests of innovators and the public, creating an environment conducive to the flourishing of creativity and innovation and ultimately benefiting society as a whole. In the current global economy, Geographical Indications are increasingly recognised as a significant form of intellectual property. Geographical Indications are currently regarded as a significant body of scholarly literature pertaining to a diverse range of products. Every society accumulates a distinct knowledge base over an extended period of time. The development of this knowledge repository can be attributed to geological circumstances and human interactions, ultimately becoming a significant component of their economy and cultural heritage.

The concept of Geographical Indication (GI) pertains to a form of intellectual property that serves to designate a product's origin to a particular geographic area. Geographical Indication (GI) products exhibit distinct qualities or characteristics that are specific to the geographic area of their production, and these attributes can be attributed to the natural or human factors present in that region. The utilisation of a Geographical Indication (GI) on a product signifies its adherence to specific standards of quality, its association with a particular reputation, and its possession of distinctive attributes that are exclusive to the geographical region from which it originates.

Geographical indications (GIs) have the potential to be utilised across a diverse array of commodities, encompassing food and agricultural products, handicrafts, as well as industrial products. Illustrations of Geographical Indication (GI) products encompass renowned items such as Champagne wine originating from France, Darjeeling tea hailing from India, and Parmigiano Reggiano cheese originating from Italy. The primary objective of geographical indication (GI) protection is to safeguard the distinctive attributes and properties of products, while also prohibiting unauthorised utilisation of the designated name or label by producers situated beyond the geographical region of origin. This measure serves to guarantee equitable trade practises, foster sustainable development, and safeguard cultural heritage.

Legal frameworks at both the national and international levels provide protection for GIs. The Agreement on Trade-Related Aspects of Intellectual Property Rights (TRIPS), established by the World Trade Organisation (WTO), serves as a legal framework for safeguarding Geographical Indications (GIs). Numerous nations have implemented legislation and regulatory measures to ensure the protection of products associated with GIs. The aforementioned laws and regulations commonly necessitate the registration of a Geographical Indication (GI) product, while also delineating the qualifying criteria, registration procedures, and mechanisms for enforcing the protection of said product.

ORIGIN OF GEOGRAPHICAL INDICATION

The notion of Geographical Indications (GI) emerged in Europe during the early 20th century as a mechanism to safeguard the designations and prestige of particular food and agricultural commodities originating from specific regions. The initial geographical indication (GI) system was instituted in France during the 1930s with the primary objective of safeguarding the designation of origin for "Roquefort" cheese. The concept of safeguarding products according to their geographical origin gained traction during the 1980s following the establishment of the Geographical Indication (GI) system by the European Union (EU). The significance of Geographical Indications (GIs) was acknowledged by the World Trade Organisation (WTO) in 1992, leading to their inclusion in the Agreement on Trade-Related Aspects of Intellectual Property Rights (TRIPS).

Subsequently, numerous nations have implemented their own Geographical Indication (GI) systems with the aim of safeguarding and advancing their respective traditional products. As an illustration, India has implemented Geographical Indication (GI) safeguards for renowned commodities like Darjeeling tea and Basmati rice, whereas Mexico has granted protection to the designation "Tequila." Currently, Geographical Indications (GIs) are widely acknowledged as a significant instrument for safeguarding and advancing traditional commodities, conserving cultural legacy, and fostering economic advantages for producers hailing from specific geographic areas. The scope of the GI system has been expanded to encompass not only food and agricultural products, but also handicrafts, wines and spirits, and various other traditional products.

The Geographical Indication (GI) system was implemented in India with the enactment of the Geographical Indications of Goods (Registration and Protection) Act in 1999. The legislation was enacted on September 15, 2003, with the purpose of establishing a framework for the registration and safeguarding of Geographical Indications (GIs) within the jurisdiction of India.

In 2004, the initial product to be officially registered as a Geographical Indication (GI) in India was Darjeeling tea. Subsequently, a number of additional products have been officially recognised and registered as Geographical Indications (GIs). These include:

1. Basmati Rice (registered in 2008) 2. Pashmina (registered in 2008) 3. Nagpur Orange (registered in 2014)

The topic of discussion is Mysore Silk, specifically focusing on the year 2005. In the year 2018, Alphonso Mango was observed.

The geographical indication (GI) system in India has been instrumental in facilitating the promotion and safeguarding of traditional products that possess distinct characteristics associated with specific regions within the country. Furthermore, this initiative has yielded economic advantages for the producers involved, as it guarantees them equitable remuneration for their goods and facilitates the promotion of said products in both domestic and international markets.

The Indian government has implemented various measures to facilitate the advancement and safeguarding of Geographical Indications (GIs) within the nation. These initiatives encompass the establishment of a specialised Geographical Indications Registry situated in Chennai, as well as the provision of financial aid to producers to support the registration and promotion of their respective products. The Geographical Indications (GI) system in India has effectively facilitated the promotion of the distinctive cultural heritage of the nation, while simultaneously playing a significant role in fostering the development of the rural economy.

UNIQUE CHARACTERISTICS OF GI PRODUCTS

Geographical Indication (GI) products are renowned for possessing distinctive attributes that can be attributed to their specific geographic origins. The aforementioned characteristics may be attributed to either natural or human factors that play a role in the production of the product. Several distinctive features can be attributed to GI (Geographical Indication) products.

Terroir encompasses the distinctive amalgamation of soil composition, climatic conditions, topographical features, and additional environmental elements that exert influence on the cultivation and calibre of a given product. Geographical indication (GI) products are frequently linked to particular terroirs, which contribute to their unique characteristics in terms of flavour, aroma, and texture.

Traditional production techniques: Numerous Geographical Indication (GI) products are manufactured employing time-honored methodologies that have been transmitted across successive generations. The aforementioned techniques may encompass distinct methods of harvesting or processing that are exclusive to the region and play a role in enhancing the quality and distinctive attributes of the product.

Utilisation of regional ingredients: Geographical Indication (GI) products frequently incorporate locally sourced ingredients that are unique to the respective area. An instance of this can be observed in the production of Parmigiano Reggiano cheese, where the milk utilised is sourced from cows that engage in grazing activities on the indigenous grasses found in the Parma region of Italy. This particular practise contributes to the distinct flavour profile that characterises the cheese

Cultural heritage is frequently intertwined with Geographical Indication (GI) products. The manufacturing of these products may exhibit a strong association with indigenous festivals, customs, or traditions, thereby enhancing their distinctiveness and renown.**Quality standards** are implemented in the production of GI products to guarantee uniformity and genuineness. The establishment of these standards can be attributed to either governmental bodies or local associations responsible for regulating the production of the respective product.

In general, the distinctive attributes of geographical indication (GI) products are intricately associated with their specific geographic origins and the inherent natural, cultural, and human elements that play a role in their manufacturing processes. The aforementioned attributes render GI products discernible and valuable, thereby facilitating the preservation and promotion of a region's distinctive cultural heritage.

REPUTATION OF GI PRODUCTS

The association between the reputation of Geographical Indication (GI) products and their geographical origin and distinctive attributes is highly interconnected. Products that possess a Geographical Indication (GI) status are frequently regarded as exhibiting superior quality and authenticity in comparison to similar products lacking such a designation. The reputation of GI products is built over time through their consistent quality, distinct flavor, aroma, texture, and other unique characteristics that are attributed to their specific region of origin.

The reputation of Geographical Indication (GI) products is also derived from the region-specific traditional production methods. The aforementioned conventional techniques are frequently transmitted across successive generations and possess profound connections to the indigenous culture and historical context. The utilisation of these conventional techniques imparts a genuine quality to the products and enhances their standing. Furthermore, the reputation of GI products is established upon the rigorous quality standards that are enforced by the governing bodies tasked with regulating their production. The implementation of these standards serves to uphold the calibre and genuineness of the products, thereby bolstering their standing.

The establishment of the reputation of GI products is further facilitated by strategic marketing and promotional endeavours, which effectively emphasise their distinctive attributes and their affiliation with a particular geographic locale. The marketing and promotional campaign serves to enhance consumer awareness regarding the product, its quality, and its origin, thereby bolstering its reputation.

The reputation of GI products is intricatly linkcd to factors such as their geographical origin, adherence to traditional production methods, stringent quality standards, and effective marketing and promotional strategies. The positive perception of GI (Geographical Indication) products plays a pivotal role in fostering consumer confidence and trust, thereby significantly influencing their commercial viability and prosperity.

LEGAL FRAMEWORK FOR GI

The legal framework governing the safeguarding of Geographical Indications (GIs) is established both domestically and internationally.

The protection of Geographical Indications (GIs) is established at the international level through the Agreement on Trade-Related Aspects of Intellectual Property Rights (TRIPS) of the World Trade Organisation (WTO). The Agreement on Trade-Related Aspects of Intellectual Property Rights (TRIPS) mandates that member nations must establish legal safeguards for geographical indications (GIs) and outlines the basic criteria for ensuring such protection. The Agreement on Trade-Related Aspects of Intellectual Property Rights (TRIPS) mandates the safeguarding of Geographical Indications (GIs) as a category of intellectual property. Additionally, it necessitates that member nations establish legal structures to facilitate the registration and preservation of GIs.

At the national level, countries have the authority to establish their own legal frameworks and regulatory measures in order to safeguard Geographical Indications (GIs). The laws and regulations pertaining to geographical indications (GIs) exhibit variability across different countries, yet their primary purpose is to establish mechanisms for the registration and safeguarding of GIs. The criteria for eligibility for geographical indication (GI) protection, the registration procedures, and the enforcement mechanisms for safeguarding the GI product are typically established by laws and regulations. Certain countries have established distinct legal frameworks to safeguard Geographical Indications (GIs), which are separate from the broader intellectual property laws. In the context of the European Union, geographical indications (GIs) receive legal protection through the EU's Regulation on the protection of geographical indications and designations of origin for agricultural products and foodstuffs. The aforementioned regulation institutes a comprehensive registration system for Geographical Indications (GIs) and delineates the specific criteria that must be met in order to qualify for GI protection.

Enforcement mechanisms aimed at safeguarding Geographical Indication (GI) protection encompass a range of measures. These measures may involve the imposition of civil and criminal penalties to address instances of infringement. Additionally, border measures can be implemented to effectively prevent the importation of products that infringe upon GI rights. Furthermore, administrative procedures are put in place to facilitate the revocation or cancellation of GI registrations when necessary. Certain nations have established dedicated organisations to supervise the registration and safeguarding of geographical indications (GIs).

In brief, the legal infrastructure pertaining to the safeguarding of geographical indications (GIs) is instituted both domestically and globally. The safeguarding of geographical indications (GIs) typically entails the formal registration of the GI product, the establishment of specific eligibility criteria, and the implementation of legal measures to ensure that producers from regions other than the designated origin refrain from using the GI label. Enforcement mechanisms encompass a range of measures, such as civil and criminal penalties, border measures, and administrative procedures aimed at revoking or cancelling the registration of Geographical Indications (GIs).

INTERNATIONAL LEGAL FRAMEWORK FOR GI PROTECTION

Understanding the four fundamental questions that encompass "why, when, where, and for what" is essential for comprehending a concept in its entirety. In a similar vein, it can be argued that the concept of geographical indication lacks comprehensiveness in the absence of responses to these inquiries. This chapter offers responses to inquiries regarding geographical indications, including their historical origins, operational mechanisms, protective measures, and the current international framework governing their utilisation and prevention of misuse. This chapter examines the historical development of geographical indications, tracing its progression from the Paris Convention on Intellectual Property in 1883 to the WTO Agreement on Trade-Related Aspects of Intellectual Property Rights in 1994. Understanding the historical development of Geographical Indications (GI) is crucial for gaining a comprehensive understanding of the legal framework and safeguards surrounding this intellectual property right. One of the primary concerns pertaining to the legal safeguarding of geographical indications is the presence of conflicts within the respective geographical regions. Therefore, similar to other components of intellectual property rights (IPR), geographical indications (GI) have also undergone numerous reforms. Despite the implementation of numerous reforms, a consensus regarding the standard procedures for gastrointestinal (GI) diseases remains elusive. The TRIPS agreement encompasses the fundamental principles that pertain to various intellectual property rights, including geographical indications. These principles primarily include the national treatment principle and the Most Favoured Nation clause.

NATIONAL TREATMENT

Article 3 of the Agreement on Trade-Related Aspects of Intellectual Property Rights (TRIPS) establishes regulations regarding national treatment, which require individuals to provide treatment to nationals of other member countries that is no less favourable than the treatment provided to their own nationals with respect to the protection of intellectual property. The national treatment rule of the TRIPS Agreement is contingent upon the exemptions provided in the Paris Convention, as stated in Article 3 of the TRIPS Agreement. Additionally, the organisation of the subject matter implies the presence of exceptions that are allowed according to the Berne and Rome Conventions.

MOST-FAVORED NATION TREATMENT

According to Article 4 of the TRIPS Agreement, in the context of safeguarding intellectual property, any form of preferential treatment, advantage, privilege, or exemption that a Member grants to the citizens of one country must be promptly and unconditionally extended to the citizens of all other Members.

The primary establishment of the international legal framework for the protection of Geographical Indications (GIs) is accomplished through the Agreement on Trade- Related Aspects of Intellectual Property Rights (TRIPS) of the World Trade Organisation (WTO). The Agreement on Trade-Related Aspects of Intellectual Property Rights (TRIPS) establishes the fundamental criteria for safeguarding and implementing Geographical Indications (GIs), mandating that all member nations of the World Trade Organisation (WTO) must offer legal safeguards for GIs.

According to the Agreement on Trade-Related Aspects of Intellectual Property Rights (TRIPS), Geographical Indications (GIs) are described as indications that serve to identify a product as originating from a particular geographical region, where the product's specific qualities, reputation, or other distinguishing characteristics are primarily linked to its geographical origin. The Agreement on Trade-Related Aspects of Intellectual Property Rights (TRIPS) mandates that member nations must extend legal safeguards to Geographical Indications (GIs) in a manner that is impartial, without discrimination based on the origin of the GI, whether it is domestic or foreign. The Agreement on Trade-Related Aspects of Intellectual Property Rights (TRIPS) mandates that member nations must afford Geographical Indications (GIs) a certain degree of legal safeguarding, which encompasses the authority to prohibit unauthorised utilisation of the GI. The Agreement on Trade-Related Aspects of Intellectual Property Rights (TRIPS) mandates that member nations must implement protocols for the registration of Geographical Indications (GIs), and it also includes provisions for the potential cancellation or revocation of a GI registration in specific situations.

The Agreement on Trade-Related Aspects of Intellectual Property Rights (TRIPS) also establishes a mechanism for resolving disputes pertaining to the protection and enforcement of geographical indications (GIs). This mechanism enables member nations to lodge a complaint against another member nation due to its failure in ensuring sufficient safeguarding measures for geographical indications (GIs). The dispute settlement mechanism encompasses provisions for potential sanctions or alternative measures in cases where a member nation is determined to have breached its obligations under the Agreement on Trade-Related Aspects of Intellectual Property Rights (TRIPS).

Besides the Agreement on Trade-Related Aspects of Intellectual Property Rights (TRIPS), there exist various other international agreements and initiatives that facilitate the safeguarding of geographical indications (GIs). An instance of this can be observed in the Lisbon Agreement for the Protection of Appellations of Origin and their International Registration, which establishes a structure for the global registration of Geographical Indications (GIs). The International Trademark Association (INTA) additionally offers guidance and best practises pertaining to the safeguarding of geographical indications (GIs).

In brief, the principal foundation for safeguarding Geographical Indications (GIs) within the global legal framework is predominantly constituted by the Agreement on Trade-Related Aspects of Intellectual Property Rights (TRIPS). This agreement mandates that all member nations of the World Trade Organisation (WTO) must furnish legal safeguards for GIs. The Agreement on Trade-Related Aspects of Intellectual Property Rights (TRIPS) outlines the fundamental criteria for safeguarding Geographical Indications (GIs) and establishes protocols for the registration and implementation of GIs. In conjunction with the Agreement on Trade-Related Aspects of Intellectual Property Rights (TRIPS), various other international agreements and initiatives exist to facilitate the safeguarding of Geographical Indications (GIs).

3.3 GEOGRAPHICAL INDICATION AND INDIA

Geographical Indication (GI) products in India represent a remarkable fusion of tradition, quality, and regional identity. These products are not merely commodities; they are cultural symbols and economic lifelines for the regions that produce them. In a nation as diverse as India, the rich tapestry of GI products reflects the country's multifaceted culture, geography, and agricultural practices. They exemplify the coexistence of modernity and tradition and are instrumental in addressing rural development, cultural preservation, and sustainable economic growth. The Geographical Indication system in India is more than just a legal framework; it is a celebration of the nation's cultural and economic heritage. India has a rich tradition of producing various products that are closely tied to specific geographical regions and possess unique qualities, characteristics, and reputations. These products are often protected under the Geographical Indication (GI) tag in India, which helps in preserving the cultural and economic significance of these items.

The GI tag in India is a powerful mechanism for preserving and promoting the country's rich and diverse cultural and economic heritage. It contributes to rural development, sustains traditional practices, and facilitates the growth of local economies, all while ensuring the authenticity and quality of products closely tied to specific geographical regions. It is a testament to the importance of place-based identities and the value of cultural and regional diversity in India.

Here are some important aspects of the GI tag in India:

1. **Legal Framework**: The Geographical Indications of Goods (Registration and Protection) Act, 1999, governs the registration and protection of geographical indications in India. This legal framework provides a foundation for the protection of products closely linked to specific geographic regions.
2. **Registration Process**: To obtain a GI tag, producers or associations need to apply to the Geographical Indications Registry, providing detailed information about the product's unique characteristics and its connection to the specific geographical area. The application goes through a rigorous review process, and if approved, the product is granted GI protection.
3. **Protection and Exclusivity**: GI registration grants producers exclusive rights to use the registered name for their products. This prevents others from using the name without proper authorization. The exclusivity helps protect the reputation and authenticity of the product.
4. **Promotion and Marketing**: The GI tag plays a crucial role in marketing and promoting products based on their regional uniqueness. It helps consumers recognize the quality and authenticity of the products and encourages their consumption and purchase.
5. **Economic Benefits**: GI products often serve as a source of income for local communities, supporting farmers, artisans, and other stakeholders. By preserving and promoting these products, the GI tag contributes to the economic well-being of these regions.
6. **International Recognition**: Many Indian GI products, such as Darjeeling tea, Basmati rice, and Kanchipuram silk sarees, enjoy international recognition and demand. The GI tag helps these products stand out in the global marketplace and protect them from imitations.
7. **Diverse Range of Products**: India boasts a wide variety of GI products, including agricultural products like rice, tea, and spices, traditional crafts like sarees and jewelry, and even regional food specialties.
8. **Enforcement**: The government and associated authorities actively monitor and enforce the protection of GI products. This ensures that the reputation and authenticity of these products are maintained.
9. **Cultural and Traditional Significance**: GI products are deeply intertwined with local culture, heritage, and traditional knowledge. They help preserve traditional craftsmanship and practices while providing a sense of identity and pride to the communities involved.

REGISTERED GEOGRAPHICAL INDICATION PRODUCTS OF INDIA

The total number of GI Tagged products registered in the respective years from 2004 to 2022 is depicted in the line chart. The curve shows a steady increase in the total GI registrations. Karnataka accounted for about 44 GI Tagged products and is renowned for the highest number of GIs in India, reflecting institutional excellence. 2008 – 2009 was recorded with peak GI registrations of agricultural, handicrafts and manufactured products. The total applications received accounted for 801, of which 417 products were registered as Geographical Indication (GI) Tagged products, 53 applications were refused, 25 were withdrawn, and 28 were abandoned. Moreover, 35 per cent

(278) of GI applications are pending.

CLASSIFICATION OF PRODUCTS

As per the Geographical Indication Act, 1999, Section – 2 (f), Traditional goods are classified as Handicrafts, Agricultural, Natural, Manufactured and Foodstuff. India is renowned for 230 Handicrafts products which account for 58 per cent of total GI Tagged Products, 131 Agricultural products, which have a share of 30 per cent, and 39 (7 per cent) manufactured products, within which about 24 products are foreign GI Tagged Products registered in India.15 (4 per cent) of the total products come under foodstuff and 2 products as natural. Out of 417 Geographical Indicated Products, Handicrafts hold the highest share of 58 per cent, the least being the natural products.

FAMOUS GEOGRAPHICAL INDICATION PRODUCTS OF INDIA

DARJEELING TEA

Darjeeling tea is a tea made from Camellia sinensis var. sinensis that is grown and processed in Darjeeling district or Kalimpong district in West Bengal, India. Since 2004, the term Darjeeling tea has been a registered geographical indication referring to products produced on certain estates within Darjeeling and Kalimpong. The tea leaves are processed as black tea, though some estates have expanded their product offerings to include leaves suitable for making green, white, and oolong teas.

The tea leaves are harvested by plucking the plant's top two leaves and the bud, from March to November, a time span that is divided into four flushes. The first flush consists of the first few leaves grown after the plant's winter dormancy and produce a light floral tea with a slight astringency; this flush is also suitable for producing a white tea. Second flush leaves are harvested after the plant has been attacked by a leafhopper and the camellia tortrix so that the leaves create a tea with a distinctive muscatel aroma. The warm and wet weather of monsoon flush rapidly produces leaves but they are less flavorful and often used for blending. The autumn flush produces teas similar to, but more muted than, the second flush.

BANARASI SARI

A Banarasi sari is a sari made in Varanasi, an ancient city which is also called Benares (Banaras). The saris are among the finest saris in India and are known for their gold and silver brocade or zari, fine silk and opulent embroidery. The saris are made of finely woven silk and are decorated with intricate designs, and, because of these engravings, are relatively heavy.A man making a handcrafted Banarasi Silk sari Their special characteristics include intricate intertwining floral and foliate motifs, kalga and bel, a string of upright leaves called jhallar at the outer, edge of border is a characteristic of these saris. Other features are gold work, compact weaving, figures with small details, metallic visual effects, pallus, jal (a net like pattern), and mina work. The saris are often part of an Indian bride's trousseau.

MYSORE SANDALWOOD OIL

Mysore Sandalwood Oil is a trademarked perfume oil extracted from the Santalum album variety of sandalwood tree (also known as a "royal tree") in the Mysore district of Karnataka, India. The tree species is said to be one of the best varieties in the world.

To preserve its importance to the economy, according to the Government Gazetteer, the government introduced special laws and regulations. In the erstwhile princely state of Mysore (part of Karnataka since independence), sandal was a "royal tree", with the state government controlling it. This oil has been registered for protection under the geographical indication of the Trade Related Intellectual Property Rights (TRIPS) agreement. In 2006, it was listed as "Mysore Sandalwood Oil" under the GI Act 1999 of the Government of India, with registration confirmed by the Controller General of Patents Designs and Trademarks.

4. BLUE POTTERY OF JAIPUR

Blue Pottery is widely recognized as a traditional craft of Jaipur of Central Asian origin. The name 'blue pottery' comes from the eye-catching cobalt blue dye used to colour the pottery. It is one of many Eurasian types of blue and white pottery, and related in the shapes and decoration to Islamic pottery and, more distantly, Chinese pottery. Jaipur blue pottery has strong influences of the Persian ceramic style but it has developed its own designs and motifs.

Inspired more from nature, the pottery is adorned with profusely animals, birds and flowers with a hint of Persian geometric design in the compositions. Some of this pottery is semi-transparent and mostly decorated with Mughal arabesque patterns and bird and other animal motifs. Thus, the semi-transparent pottery has a gentle mix of Mughal arabesque patterns with bird and other animal motifs forbidden in Persian art of Islamic origin.

5. KASHMIR SAFFRON

Kashmir saffron, which is cultivated and harvested in the Karewa (highlands) of Jammu and Kashmir, has been given the Geographical Indication (GI) tag by the Geographical Indications Registry. The spice is grown in some regions of Kashmir, including Pulwama, Budgam, Kishtwar and Srinagar. Kashmir saffron is renowned globally as a spice. It rejuvenates health and is used in cosmetics and for medicinal purposes. It has been associated with traditional Kashmiri cuisine and represents the rich cultural heritage of the region. The unique characteristics of Kashmir saffron are its longer and thicker stigmas, natural deep-red colour, high aroma, bitter flavour, chemical-free processing, and high quantity of crocin (colouring strength), safranal (flavour) and picrocrocin (bitterness). The application was filed by the Directorate of Agriculture, Government of Jammu and Kashmir, and facilitated by the Sher-e-Kashmir University of Agriculture Sciences and Technology, Kashmir, and Saffron Research Station, Dussu (Pampore).

6. SALEM FABRIC

Salem fabric likely refers to textiles or fabrics produced in Salem, a city located in the southern Indian state of Tamil Nadu. Salem is known for its textile industry, and it is particularly famous for the production of a fabric called "Salem Fabric" or "Salem Silk. The silk fabric is often soft, lustrous, and has a smooth texture. It is often used in the making of sarees, traditional clothing, and other garments. Salem fabric, particularly Salem Silk, is commonly used for bridal attire, traditional Indian clothing, and special occasions due to its sheen, texture, and elegance. Within Salem Silk, there are different types and qualities of silk, such as the Salem Venpattu silk and Salem Pattu silk. These variations are known for their specific characteristics.

7. THANJAVUR DOLL

The Thanjavur doll is a type of traditional Indian bobblehead or roly-poly toy made of terracotta material. The centre of gravity and total weight of the doll is concentrated at its bottom-most point, generating a dance-like continuous movement with slow oscillations. These toys are traditionally handmade, finished with detailed, painted exteriors. They have been recognized as a Geographical Indication by the Government of India as of 2008-09.

8. MYSORE SILK

The Mysore Silk sarees are one of the finest forms of sarees which is very popular across the globe. It comes in vibrant colors and gives a rich feel and a classic look to the saree. Like the Kancheepuram silk sarees the Mysore silk saree are also an innate form of the culture and the tradition of the people of both South and North India. The varieties of the Mysore silk sarees are compared in par with that of the world famous Kancheepuram sarees thereby topping the list. The origin of Mysore silk saree is from Karnataka and is supposed to be one of the purest forms of silk. It adds to one of the unique features of Karnataka and attracts customers from different parts of the country. The first Mysore Silk factory was started by the Maharaja of Mysore province in the year 1912 and effectively got into production in the year 1932.

3.2.4 LEGAL FRAMEWORK FOR GI PROTECTION IN INDIA

India possesses a well-developed legal framework that effectively safeguards Geographical Indications (GIs). The primary establishment of the legal framework for the protection of Geographical Indications (GIs) in India is facilitated by the Geographical Indications of Goods (Registration and Protection) Act, 1999, along with its accompanying rules and regulations.

The Geographical Indications of Goods (Registration and Protection) Act of 1999 provides a definition for Geographical Indications (GIs) as indications that serve to identify goods as originating or being manufactured within a specific country, region, or locality

within that country. These indications are used when a particular quality, reputation, or other characteristic of the goods can be primarily attributed to their geographical origin. The legislation facilitates the registration and safeguarding of Geographical Indications (GIs) within the jurisdiction of India. The legislation facilitates the creation of a Geographical Indications Registry, which assumes the responsibility of registering Geographical Indications. The legislation additionally outlines the conditions for qualifying for geographical indication (GI) protection. These conditions encompass the necessity for the GI to be linked to a distinct geographic area and for the product's quality or attributes to be primarily derived from its geographical origin.

The legislation stipulates the conditions under which a Geographical Indication (GI) registration may be cancelled or revoked. These circumstances include instances where the GI no longer maintains its association with the region of origin or when it is utilised in a manner that deceives consumers regarding the actual source of the product. In addition to the legal safeguards offered by the Geographical Indications of Goods (Registration and Protection) Act of 1999, Geographical Indications (GIs) in India are also afforded protection under the Trademarks Act of 1999. According to the Trademarks Act of 1999, Geographical Indications (GIs) are classified as a form of trademark and are afforded equivalent legal safeguards as other trademarks.

In India, the legal framework for the protection of Geographical Indications (GIs) is further reinforced by various additional legislations and regulations. One such legislation is the Food Safety and Standards Act of 2006, which facilitates the regulation of food products and aims to prevent deceptive claims. Additionally, the Customs Act of 1962 empowers the authorities to seize and eliminate goods that violate GIs at the country's borders.

In conclusion, India possesses a comprehensive legal framework aimed at safeguarding Geographical Indications (GIs). This framework encompasses the Geographical Indications of Goods (Registration and Protection) Act, 1999, the Trademarks Act, 1999, and various other legislations and regulatory measures. The existing legal framework encompasses provisions for the registration and safeguarding of geographical indications (GIs), along with provisions for the potential cancellation or revocation of GI registrations in specific

circumstances. The legal framework in India has been strategically formulated to safeguard the interests of Geographical Indication (GI) product producers and to effectively curb any instances of misappropriation or unauthorised utilisation of GI labels.

5. ENFORCEMENT OF GI PROTECTION IN INDIA

The protection and enforcement of Geographical Indications (GIs) in India are implemented through a range of legal and administrative mechanisms.

The Geographical Indications of Goods (Registration and Protection) Act of 1999 facilitates the implementation of measures to safeguard Geographical Indications (GIs) by means of both civil and criminal legal proceedings. The legislation encompasses various civil remedies, including injunctions, damages, and accounts of profits, that can be pursued by the duly registered proprietor of a geographical indication (GI) against any individual who commits an infringement upon the registered GI. The legislation additionally encompasses provisions for punitive measures in cases of unpermitted utilisation of a duly registered geographical indication (GI), encompassing potential imprisonment and monetary penalties.

The legislation additionally includes provisions for the creation of a Geographical Indications Registry, which assumes the responsibility of registering geographical indications (GIs) and maintaining a record of the registered GIs. The authority vested in the Registry enables it to invalidate or withdraw a Geographical Indication (GI) registration in instances where the GI no longer fulfils the prescribed criteria for eligibility or is employed in a manner that deceives consumers regarding the authentic source of the product. In addition to the legal enforcement mechanisms stipulated by the Act, the Indian government has also implemented various administrative mechanisms to safeguard Geographical Indications (GIs). The establishment of a National Committee on Geographical Indications (GI) by the Ministry of Commerce and Industry in India exemplifies the government's commitment to the advancement and safeguarding of GIs within the country. The Committee additionally offers support and guidance to geographical indication (GI) producers regarding a range of matters pertaining to the protection of GIs.

The Indian government engages in partnerships with a range of international organisations and foreign governments in order to enhance the safeguarding of Geographical Indications (GIs). India is a participant of the World Trade Organisation (WTO), an

international organisation that establishes a structure for safeguarding Geographical Indications (GIs) on a global scale. India is a participating party to the Agreement on Trade- Related Aspects of Intellectual Property Rights (TRIPS), which mandates member nations to establish legal safeguards for geographical indications (GIs).

In brief, the implementation of geographical indication (GI) protection in India is accomplished through a range of legal and administrative measures. These include the initiation of civil and criminal actions under the Geographical Indications of Goods (Registration and Protection) Act of 1999, the potential annulment or withdrawal of GI registrations by the Geographical Indications Registry, and the formation of administrative entities like the National Committee on GI. The Indian government engages in partnerships with international organisations and foreign governments in order to enhance the safeguarding of Geographical Indications (GIs) on a global scale.

6. CHALLENGES AND OPPORTUNITIES FOR GI PROTECTION

The protection of Geographical Indications (GIs) poses a range of challenges and opportunities for producers, consumers, and governments alike.

One of the primary obstacles encountered in the realm of geographical indication (GI) protection pertains to the effective implementation of legal measures aimed at safeguarding against unauthorised use or infringement. In numerous nations, particularly those in the process of development, the implementation of intellectual property rights may exhibit deficiencies, resulting in extensive violations of geographical indications. The aforementioned circumstance can lead to a decline in financial earnings for producers and a deterioration of the reputation associated with the products affiliated with the Geographical Indication (GI).

One additional obstacle pertains to the financial burden associated with acquiring geographical indication (GI) protection, a factor that may pose significant barriers for producers operating on a smaller scale. The acquisition of geographical indication (GI) protection entails a series of legal and administrative procedures, encompassing the identification of the specific GI, documentation of its distinctive attributes, and the subsequent submission of an application to the pertinent governing bodies. The expenses linked to these procedures can pose a substantial obstacle for producers operating on a small scale.

Nevertheless, geographical indication (GI) protection also offers various prospects for producers, consumers, and governments. Geographical Indication (GI) protection can serve as a valuable tool for producers in establishing a distinct identity for their products and effectively distinguishing them from comparable offerings within the market. This phenomenon can lead to a rise in demand, an increase in prices, and enhanced livelihoods for producers.

Geographical Indication (GI) protection offers consumers a sense of certainty regarding the calibre and legitimacy of a product, thereby bolstering consumer trust and fostering consumer allegiance. Geographical Indication (GI) protection can also serve the purpose of safeguarding traditional knowledge and practises that are intrinsically linked to the production of a particular product. This preservation effort can significantly contribute to the cultural heritage of a specific region.

Governments can utilise geographical indication (GI) protection as a means to facilitate economic development through the facilitation of local industry expansion and the generation of employment prospects. Geographical Indication (GI) protection can also facilitate international trade by facilitating the exportation of products and cultivating a favourable perception of the country of origin.

Geographical Indication (GI) protection poses various challenges and opportunities for producers, consumers, and governments alike. Although the acquisition of geographical indication (GI) protection and the enforcement of legal safeguards may present difficulties, it is important to recognise that GI protection can yield several benefits. These advantages include bolstering the reputation and economic viability of the product, as well as fostering the preservation of cultural heritage and facilitating international trade.

7. GEOGRAPHICAL INDICATION AND RURAL DEVELOPMENT

The superior quality of products bearing a Geographical Indication (GI) tag is indisputable. The quality of the product is ensured by the GI. As a result of this guarantee, there has been a notable rise in the demand for GI products in the market. Additionally, there has been a rise in the market value of the products. In contemporary times, consumers predominantly prioritise the quality of the products they purchase. If the product demonstrates quality, they are prepared to make a payment. From a consumer's perspective,

geographical indication (GI) guarantees that a specific product is produced using traditional methods and adheres to established standards. For instance, Darjeeling tea, cultivated in the Darjeeling district of West Bengal, is preferred over other teas due to its association with the region of origin and its distinctive qualities and characteristics. Consequently, this phenomenon enhances the likelihood of facilitating the entry of domestic goods into the global marketplace. The economic valuation of geographical indications (GI) can be determined by examining the commercial exchange of products that bear a GI designation. According to a consumer study sponsored by the European Commission, it has been found that 40% of individuals express a willingness to pay a higher premium for products that possess verifiable proof of origin. From an economic perspective, wines and spirits are considered to be the most valuable products within the category of Geographical Indication (GI) products. The region plays a significant role in the context of product placement within the domain of Geographic Information (GI). The aforementioned initiative has the potential to make a significant contribution to the holistic development of rural regions. It has the capacity to generate revenue and augment the overall price of the products. The phenomenon of employment creation serves as a deterrent to the migration of rural populations to urban areas in pursuit of employment opportunities. The concept of geographic information (GI) can also be interconnected with the field of tourism. The aforementioned phenomenon not only contributes to the appreciation of the region's worth but also has the potential to enhance the quality of life for the rural community. When effectively managed, the use of graphic imagery (GI) has the potential to significantly contribute to the establishment and development of a strong brand identity. Therefore, Geographic Information (GI) plays a crucial role in enabling the establishment of versatile platforms for rural development. The subsequent illustration delineates the transformative impact of Pochampally silks on the socio-economic conditions of a rural community situated in the Telangana state of India. The Pochampally Ikat is a traditional Indian saree that originates from the region of Bhoodan Pochampally, located in the state of Telangana, India. The product was granted a Geographical Indication (GI) tag in 2004. Subsequently, the economic worth of these sarees has experienced a significant increase. The periods prior to and following the Global Financial Crisis (GI) indicate a notable 12% rise in the year 2009. The overall sales turnover has experienced a decline of 5%. Consequently, the rate of employment has

increased by 10%. Prominent corporations such as Air India, Reliance Trends, and Pantaloon have initiated the process of acquiring goods and services. Therefore, Geographic Information (GI) has the potential to enhance a nation's economic growth through the advancement of rural communities.

3.4 GEOGRAPHICAL INDICATION AND KERALA

Kerala is a geographically situated state in the southern region of India, specifically along the Malabar coast. The region is renowned for its tranquil backwaters, verdant forests, and picturesque coastlines. Kerala possesses a significant cultural legacy and is frequently acknowledged as "God's Own Country." The state possesses a populace of roughly 35 million individuals and encompasses a landmass spanning approximately 38,863 square kilometres. Kerala is geographically delineated by the Arabian Sea to the west, the Eastern Ghats to the east, and the neighbouring states of Karnataka and Tamil Nadu to the south and east, respectively. The climate of the state is characterised as tropical, featuring substantial monsoon precipitation occurring between the months of June and September, and relatively arid winters spanning from December to February.

Kerala exhibits a commendable level of literacy, boasting a literacy rate of 96.2%. Malayalam is designated as the official language of the state, with English being commonly utilised for communication purposes. The state exhibits a heterogeneous economic landscape, characterised by a range of industries including tourism, agriculture, fishing, and manufacturing, all of which make notable contributions to its gross domestic product (GDP). Kerala is renowned for its elevated human development index, and the state's social welfare endeavours are frequently regarded as exemplars for other states to emulate. Kerala possesses a culturally significant culinary heritage, characterised by a diverse assortment of gastronomic creations that exemplify the distinctive flavours and ingredients indigenous to the region. The culinary traditions of the state are significantly shaped by its proximity to the coast, resulting in a prominent incorporation of seafood as a fundamental component in numerous gastronomic preparations. Kerala is renowned for its assortment of spices, including globally exported varieties such as black pepper, cardamom, and cinnamon.

Kerala boasts a thriving arts and culture milieu, characterised by the presence of traditional music and dance genres like Kathakali and Mohiniyattam, which are widely showcased across the region. The state is renowned for its cultural festivals, including

Onam, a significant celebration that occurs in either August or September, symbolising the culmination of the harvest season. Kerala is characterised by a plethora of cultural traditions, a varied economic landscape, and awe-inspiring natural landscapes. The aforementioned location is widely recognised as a favoured choice among tourists and is characterised by its ongoing advancements and pioneering efforts across diverse domains.

The Geographical Indication (GI) tag has played a crucial role in safeguarding and promoting the distinctive products originating from Kerala, which possess significant cultural and historical value. The implementation of Geographical Indication (GI) protection has effectively established the reputation of these products as distinguished by their superior quality and distinctiveness, consequently enabling them to maintain a competitive advantage in both domestic and international markets, thereby justifying their ability to command a higher price.

The Alleppey Green Cardamom is renowned for its distinctive taste and fragrance, and it is cultivated in the Kottayam, Idukki, and Pathanamthitta regions of Kerala. The cultivation of Wayanad Robusta Coffee takes place in the Wayanad district of Kerala, renowned for its distinctive and robust taste profile as well as its aromatic qualities. Malabar Pepper is cultivated in the Malabar region of Kerala, renowned for its robust and highly aromatic taste profile. Palakkadan Matta Rice is a conventional strain of rice cultivated in the Palakkad district of Kerala, renowned for its nutritional composition and palatability.

The implementation of Geographical Indication (GI) protection has played a pivotal role in fostering the promotion of distinctive products from Kerala, while concurrently facilitating the advancement of sustainable agricultural practises within the region. The geographical indication (GI) tag has additionally played a crucial role in safeguarding the customary knowledge and methodologies employed by the communities involved in the production of these goods, thereby making a significant contribution to the socio- cultural advancement of the area.

In general, the implementation of Geographical Indication (GI) protection has emerged as a noteworthy advancement for the distinctive products originating from the region of Kerala. The aforementioned measures have been instrumental in safeguarding

and advancing the visibility of these commodities, thereby guaranteeing their acknowledgement for their superior standards and distinctive attributes. The geographical indication (GI) tag has additionally facilitated the promotion of sustainable agricultural practises and has made significant contributions to the socio-cultural advancement of the region.

3.4.1 FAMOUS GEOGRAPHICAL INDICATION PRODUCTS OF KERALA

Kerala boasts a total of 32 products that have been officially bestowed with the esteemed Geographical Indication (GI) status. This recognition serves to acknowledge and authenticate the distinctive characteristics and provenance of these products, firmly establishing their association with specific regions within the state. Alleppey Green Cardamom, a widely recognised spice, is cultivated in the Kottayam, Idukki, and Pathanamthitta districts of Kerala.

The coffee is renowned for its distinctive flavour and aroma, and its geographical indication (GI) designation safeguards its exceptional quality and esteemed standing. The Geographical Indication (GI) of Kerala primarily pertains to agricultural products, handicraft textile products, traditional manufacturing, and traditional knowledge.

1. ARANMULA KANNADI

The Aranmula Kannadi is an exquisite mirror that has been meticulously crafted by hand in the region of Kerala, India for numerous centuries. The object is composed of a unique metallic alloy and possesses a meticulously polished surface that exhibits exceptional reflectivity, resulting in the projection of images with remarkable clarity. The item is highly regarded as a valuable heirloom and esteemed possession in numerous households, owing to its scarcity and meticulous artistry. Nevertheless, it is imperative to exercise caution when considering the practise of custom engraving in relation to Aranmula Kannadi. Although custom engraving may initially appear to enhance the aesthetic appeal of this exquisite piece, it can ultimately diminish its inherent beauty and intrinsic value.

One of the primary rationales for discouraging the practise of custom engraving on Aranmula Kannadi pertains to the potential harm it may inflict upon the mirror's intricate surface. The attainment of a mirror's polished surface is accomplished through a multifaceted and intricate procedure that encompasses the utilisation of conventional methodologies and substances. The process of custom engraving has the potential to modify the mirror's initial design, thereby diminishing its aesthetic appeal. The Aranmula Kannadi is renowned for its elaborate and aesthetically pleasing patterns that have been transmitted through successive generations. The process of custom engraving has the potential to conceal or diminish the visual appeal of these designs, thereby reducing the overall aesthetic value and monetary worth of the mirror.

2. MARAYOOR JAGGERY

The traditional sharkara possesses several distinctive characteristics, including a pronounced sweetness devoid of any salty taste, a notable iron content, reduced sodium levels, minimal insoluble impurities, an organic production method, and a deep brown coloration. According to popular belief, the region of Marayoor in Kerala possesses a historical lineage that can be traced back to the era of the Mahabharata. It is said that during their period of exile known as vanavasam, the Pandavas sought refuge in this area, leading to its designation as Maranjirunnayoor, denoting "the place of hiding." Over time, this appellation gradually transformed into the present-day name of Marayoor.

In the early stages, there was a significant emphasis on rice cultivation, leading to the region being referred to as the primary rice-producing area in the high ranges. However, as a result of water scarcity concerns, there was a shift towards cultivating sugarcane, a crop that demands less water. Presently, the cultivation is predominantly carried out by agricultural workers hailing from Tamil Nadu or individuals affiliated with the Muthuva tribal community.

3. PALAKKADAN MATTA RICE

The indigenous Palakkadan Matta rice, cultivated in the verdant region of Palakkad for centuries, stands as a renowned Geographical Indication Product of Kerala. Historians assert that the consumption of Matta rice was limited exclusively to the royal households of the Cholas and Cheras. The cultivation of this particular variety of rice was limited to the exclusive use of the royal households, which maintained extensive gardens for this purpose. On a fortuitous occasion, an inquisitive agriculturalist encountered a specimen and proceeded to extract a sample, which was subsequently utilised for cultivation on the individual's property. Undoubtedly, this assortment was enjoyed by all and swiftly supplanted the frequently utilised chama rice that was consumed by the individuals. Subsequently, the aforementioned variety of rice acquired the appellation "Matta rice." The rice variety under consideration is predominantly cultivated in the region of Palakkad, thus earning the nomenclature of Palakkadan Matta rice. The agricultural and climatic factors found in Palakkad, such as the presence of black cotton soil with high lime, potash, magnesium, and calcium carbonate content, as well as the poonthalpadam soil characterised by 60–80 percent clay and silt, low permeability, and high water retention capacity, along with the humid weather conditions, easterly winds passing through the Palakkad Gap, abundant sunshine, and the water supply from rivers originating in the Western Ghats, create highly favourable conditions for cultivating this particular type of rice. The cultivation of rice relies solely on traditional methods that have been passed down through generations.

4. KUTHAMPULLY SAREE

The Kuthampully Saree is a variant of the traditional Indian garment known as the Sari. It is produced by skilled weavers hailing from the village of Kuthampully, located in the Thiruvilwamala Grama Panchayat of the Thrissur district in the state of Kerala, India. The Kuthampully Saree is characterised by its distinctive saree borders. The Kuthampully Handloom Industrial Cooperative Society was officially registered in 1972, boasting a membership of 102 individuals. Currently, the organisation boasts a membership of 814 individuals and possesses a dedicated establishment located in Kuthampully. The Kuthampully Saree was granted exclusive Intellectual Property rights under the Geographical Indication Act (GI) in September 2011. The historical lineage of the Kuthampully Sarees and other high-quality cotton textiles from Kerala can be traced back to the late 18th century CE, as these products are intricately linked to the Royal family of Kochi. According to historical records, it is documented that the Devanga Chettiar community, known for their expertise in traditional weaving, originated from the region of Mysore in the present-day state of Karnataka. These skilled weavers were specifically invited by the Kochi Royal family to engage in the exclusive production of dress materials for the palace. According to historical accounts, it is widely held that the Devanga Chettis, originating from Mysore, migrated from their homeland due to the persecution inflicted upon them by Tipu Sultan. Subsequently, they established their settlement in a remote village in the latter part of the eighteenth century.

5. VAZHAKULAM PINEAPPLE

Vazhakulam serves as the primary hub for pineapple trade in the state of Kerala, contributing approximately 80% of Kerala's pineapple harvest that is distributed throughout the entire country. The Vazhakulam pineapple plantation is situated within the Vazhakulam Panchayat, which falls under the administrative jurisdiction of the Muvattapuzha division. It is approximately one hour's drive from Kochi in the Ernakulam district. The mean weight of fruit falls within the range of 1300 to 1600 grammes. The fruit possesses a delightful fragrance, exhibiting a slightly conical shape with its fruit "eyes" deeply embedded. The flesh of the fruit is firm and displays a vibrant golden yellow hue. The juice extracted from the fruit is characterised by its sweetness, measuring between 14-160 brix, while its acidity ranges from 0.50 to 0.70%. This particular source is deemed to be rich in carotene, vitamins, and minerals.

The socio-cultural history of Vazhakulam commenced during the 1940s through the initiation of a modest-scale production. Nevertheless, due to the advantageous climate conditions, the enterprise transitioned into a commercial endeavour within a decade.

The Vazakulam pineapple exhibits a shelf life ranging from 15 to 20 days, during which it is suitable for consumption as a fresh fruit. The cultivation of this crop spans across an area of 10,000 hectares, encompassing the districts of Ernakulam, Kottayam, and certain regions of Pathanamthitta district, as well as the lower regions of Idukki district. Vazhakulam holds the distinction of being the largest pineapple market in India, boasting a track record of over 15 years of exceptional performance. In 2009, the fruit was granted a Geographical Indication (GI) tag. The fruit possesses a delightful fragrance and exhibits a slightly conical shape. Its flesh is characterised by a highly crisp texture and a vibrant golden yellow hue. Due to its elevated sugar content, this particular product has gained considerable popularity for domestic consumption.

6. KAIPAD RICE

Kaipad rice cultivation refers to the longstanding practise of cultivating organic rice in the saline-prone coastal rice tracts located in the northern districts of Kerala, namely Kozhikode, Kannur, and Kasaragod. The Geographical Indication (GI) registration certificate for Kaipad rice was acquired on March 3, 2014.A total area of approximately 3400 hectares of Kaipad rice fields has been identified in Kannur district. The land area in Kozhikode district is approximately 500 hectares, while in Kasaragod district it is approximately 200 hectares. These regions have a historical reputation for their cultivation of rice.

The historical records of Dr. Francis Buchanan, an English employee of the East India Company, contain references to rice tracts in the ancient literature pertaining to the region. The rice tracts are referred to as 'KayalKandoms' and the local farmers are referred to as 'kuttadan'. The contemporary designation of 'Kaipad' is etymologically derived from the term 'Kayalpadam', wherein 'Kayal' signifies inland water bodies and 'padam' denotes cultivated fields for rice cultivation.

The majority of cultivators are characterised as small-scale and economically disadvantaged farmers. However, the cultivation practises employed in Kaipad rice tracts adhere strictly to a natural approach, relying primarily on the monsoon rains and sea tides. Rice cultivation occurs in a low to medium saline phase of the production cycle, wherein a singular crop is cultivated on mounds between the months of June and October. Traditional aquaculture practises, specifically fish or prawn farming, are implemented in these areas during the high saline phase spanning from November to April. The cultivation of rice, fish, and prawns is conducted using traditional organic methods, abstaining from the application of chemical fertilisers or pesticides. Rice possesses exceptional nutritional properties, rendering it highly sought after and commanding a premium price in the market, owing to its distinct flavour and nutritional composition. A local tradition exists among Kaipad rice cultivators wherein they present rice flakes as gifts during their visits to households located beyond their respective regions.

7. NILAMBUR TEAK

The Nilambur Teak has been granted the distinction of being the inaugural forest produce in the nation to receive a Geographical Indication (GI) tag. Nilambur teak refers to the type of teak wood that is obtained from various sources such as forest areas, plantations, and homesteads located in Nilambur Taluk and Edavanna panchayat within the Ernad Taluk of the Malappuram district in the state of Kerala. The presence of abundant alluvial deposits along the river banks of the Chaliyar river contributes to the enrichment of soil fertility, thereby augmenting the overall quality of Nilambur teak.

8. CHENDAMANGLAM DHOTIES

Chendamangalam is a tiny hamlet on the shores of the river Periyar, 30 kilometres from Ernakulam, the state capital. It is a flourishing hub of commerce and interchange close to the ancient port of Muriris. This location is also known as the birthplace of Malabari Jews, although basic materials now originate from Surat, Gujarat. However, Chendamangalam weavers are renowned for their ability to create exquisite mundus and dhotis using their hadlooms. Weavers from Andhra Pradesh and Tamil Nadu founded this textile centre. Padmashliyars, chaliyars, and bhattarayars are members of the textile community who have practised their craft for generations. Chendamangalam is famous for its set mundus, which became a useful source of employment after the Travancore Cochin Societies Act of 1955 and the formation of the cooperative Society. Cottom The grain from Gugarat is soaked in water for 24 hours to remove impurities and chemical residue before being heated at 200 degrees Celsius for improved finishing. Then they are rinsed again,

oxidised to achieve the desired hues, and left to dry in the sun for one day and three days. After each step, the fabric is placed on handloom mills. This community is comprised of approximately 10,000 weavers, 4,000 to 5,000 households, and the gramme Panchayat's population.

9. TIRUR BETEL LEAF

Tirur Betel Leaf refers to a specific variety of betel leaf that is cultivated in the region of Tirur and its surrounding areas within the Malappuram district. This is commonly referred to as the "Green Gold of India." The block panchayats of Tirur, Tanur, Tirurangadi, Kuttippuram, Malappuram, and Vengara in the Malappuram District are renowned for their cultivation of Tirur betel leaf. The Midland area, characterised by a predominantly U-shaped geography, is situated between the coastal plains to the west and the Western Ghats to the east. This region is known for its red laterite soil, which offers conducive conditions for the cultivation of Tirur Betel Leaf.

3. ECONOMIC AND SOCIAL IMPACT OF GEOGRAPHICAL INDICATION ON KERALA

Geographical Indication (GI) is a legal mechanism employed to safeguard the designations or symbols associated with commodities and merchandise derived from a distinct geographic area. In the state of Kerala, a number of products have been bestowed with Geographical Indication (GI) status. These products include Malabar Pepper, Wayanad Robusta Coffee, Alleppey Green Cardamom, and Palakkadan Matta Rice. This section examines the economic and social ramifications of Geographic Information (GI) on the state of Kerala.
ECONOMIC IMPACT

1. **Promotes Rural Economy:** One significant economic impact of Geographical Indication (GI) tags is the promotion of rural economies. This is achieved through facilitating market access and enabling higher prices for products that possess distinct characteristics. The cultivation of products such as Malabar Pepper, Alleppey Green Cardamom, and Palakkadan Matta Rice in Kerala is predominantly carried out by small- scale and subsistence farmers residing in the rural regions of the state. Geographical Indication (GI) tags facilitate enhanced market accessibility for farmers, enabling them to obtain more favourable prices for their agricultural products. Consequently, this contributes to the amelioration of their livelihoods.

2. **Increases Exports:** GI tags have the potential to enhance the exportation of products possessing distinctive attributes. Kerala is renowned for its export of high-demand products, including Malabar Pepper, Wayanad Robusta Coffee, and Alleppey Green Cardamom, which enjoy substantial popularity in the global market. Geographical Indication (GI) tags play a crucial role in safeguarding the genuineness of products and enhancing their export prospects, thereby contributing to the generation of foreign exchange for the respective region.

3. **Enhances Branding:** GI tags have the potential to enhance the branding of products that possess distinctive characteristics. Kerala is renowned for its distinctively flavoured and high-quality products, including Malabar Pepper, Alleppey Green Cardamom, and Palakkadan Matta Rice. Geographical Indication (GI) tags serve the purpose of distinguishing these products from comparable offerings in the market, thereby augmenting their branding potential and subsequently fostering an upsurge in consumer demand.

SOCIAL IMPACT:

1. **Preservation of Traditional Knowledge:** One significant social impact of Geographical Indication (GI) tags is the safeguarding of traditional knowledge and practises linked to the creation of distinctive products. Traditional methods are employed in the production of various products in Kerala, including Wayanad Robusta Coffee and Palakkadan Matta Rice. The Geographical Indication (GI) tags serve the purpose of safeguarding these customary practises and guaranteeing their preservation in the face of modernization.

2. **Empowerment of Women:** The utilisation of Geographical Indication (GI) tags has the potential to facilitate the empowerment of women residing in rural areas. This is achieved by offering them opportunities to engage in the production and marketing of products that possess distinctive characteristics. In the state of Kerala,

the cultivation and processing of products such as Alleppey Green Cardamom and Palakkadan Matta Rice are predominantly carried out by women. The Geographical Indication (GI) tags play a crucial role in facilitating market access for these women and ensuring equitable remuneration for their products, thereby contributing to the enhancement of their socio-economic standing.

3. **Cultural Identity:** The promotion of cultural identity can be facilitated by GI tags, as they serve to emphasise the distinctiveness of a particular place through the recognition of its unique products and practises. The state of Kerala boasts a rich cultural heritage, encompassing various products that hold significant value. Notable among these are Malabar Pepper, Wayanad Robusta Coffee, and Alleppey Green Cardamom. The utilisation of Geographical Indication (GI) tags serves as a means to enhance the promotion of these products and practises, thereby contributing to the preservation of the cultural identity associated with the state.

In summary, the effects of GI on the economy and society of Kerala are substantial. The Geographical Indication (GI) tags play a pivotal role in stimulating rural economies, bolstering export activities, strengthening brand recognition, safeguarding traditional knowledge and practises, empowering women, and fostering cultural identity. Hence, it is imperative to prioritise the promotion and safeguarding of Geographical Indications (GI) in the state of Kerala, as it plays a crucial role in fostering sustainable development.

4. CHALLENGES AND OPPORTUNITIES IN GEOGRAPHICAL INDICATION

PROTECTION IN KERALA

The implementation of Geographical Indication (GI) protection has presented notable prospects for the distinctive agricultural products of Kerala. However, it has also brought forth certain challenges. The following discourse highlights the various challenges and opportunities associated with Geographical Indication (GI) protection for products originating from the region of Kerala.

Challenges:

1. **Lack of awareness:** One of the primary challenges faced by small-scale producers is a lack of awareness regarding the protection offered by Geographical Indications (GIs) and the potential benefits it can bring to their products. Insufficient knowledge regarding the registration procedure, legal framework, and advantages associated with Geographical Indication (GI) protection has the potential to impede the progress and advancement of the respective products.

2. **Cost of registration:** The registration fee for Geographical Indication (GI) can be substantial, posing a potential obstacle for small-scale producers who may face financial constraints in pursuing the registration process. The potential consequence of this is a potential reduction in the range of products that can derive advantages from geographical indication (GI) protection.

3. **Enforcement:** The enforcement of geographical indication (GI) protection poses challenges, particularly in instances involving unauthorised utilisation or replication of the product. The limited resources available to small-scale producers may hinder their ability to effectively monitor and enforce the protection of their products, potentially leading to instances of infringement and dilution of their geographical indication (GI) status.

Opportunities:

1. **Market recognition:** Geographical Indication (GI) protection offers a means of establishing market recognition for the distinctive products originating from Kerala, thereby enhancing their reputation in both domestic and international markets. The acknowledgment of this phenomenon has the potential to result in increased consumer demand and improved pricing for the products in question.

2. **TheprotectionofGeographicalIndications:** (GIs) can contribute to the preservation of traditional knowledge and practises associated with the production of specific products, benefiting the communities involved. This has the potential to facilitate the socio-cultural advancement of the region and foster the adoption of sustainable agricultural methodologies.

3. **Value addition:** The protection of Geographical Indications (GI) can facilitate the exploration of new processing techniques, packaging methods, and branding strategies, thereby creating opportunities for enhancing the value of the products. This phenomenon has the potential to enhance the value of the products and yield advantages for the producers.

4. **Tourism:** The presence of distinctive products from Kerala, safeguarded by Geographical Indication (GI) protection, has the potential to draw tourists to the area, thereby generating economic prospects for the local community and facilitating the dissemination of traditional practises and cultural heritage within the region.

In summary, it can be concluded that the implementation of GI protection presents considerable prospects for the distinctive agricultural products originating from Kerala. However, certain obstacles are evident in terms of raising awareness, managing costs, and ensuring effective enforcement. Addressing these challenges necessitates the provision of governmental assistance, the implementation of educational initiatives, and the execution of awareness campaigns, alongside the establishment of strategic alliances with pertinent stakeholders. The potential benefits arising from the implementation of Geographical Indication (GI) protection for products originating from Kerala have the capacity to significantly contribute to the overall economic, social, and cultural advancement of the region.

5. CONSUMER BUYING BEHAVIOR

Consumer buying behaviour pertains to the cognitive and behavioural processes through which individuals or households arrive at decisions regarding the acquisition of goods or services. The aforementioned process is subject to a multitude of influences, encompassing psychological, social, cultural, and personal factors. Psychological factors encompass a range of individual elements such as motivations, attitudes, beliefs, and cognitive processes involved in the perception and processing of information. For instance, an individual may engage in the act of purchasing a specific product due to their perception that it will effectively fulfil a specific requirement or as a result of their favourable associations with the associated brand. Social factors encompass the impact of familial, peer, and other affiliative networks on the decision-making process of individuals regarding their purchases. As an illustration, an individual may engage in the act of purchasing a

product due to its popularity within their social circle or as a result of receiving a commendation from a familial or friendly acquaintance. Cultural factors encompass the influence of cultural values, norms, and beliefs on the decision-making process of individuals in relation to their purchasing behaviours. An individual may choose to acquire a product due to its affiliation with a specific cultural or social identity or because it aligns with their personal values or beliefs. Personal factors encompass various individual characteristics, including but not limited to age, gender, income, and lifestyle. For instance, consumers may choose to acquire a particular product based on its alignment with their age, gender, or lifestyle inclinations or due to its affordability within their financial constraints. The consumer decision-making process generally encompasses five sequential stages, namely problem recognition, information retrieval, assessment of alternatives, purchase determination, and post-purchase evaluation. During each stage, individuals may be subject to various influences and exhibit distinct patterns of behaviour. Business enterprises have the ability to employ diverse marketing tactics in order to exert an impact on consumer purchasing patterns. These strategies encompass advertising, personal selling, public relations, and sales promotion. Nevertheless, it is imperative for enterprises to take ethical considerations into account and guarantee that their marketing strategies adhere to social responsibility. The advent of the internet and social media has had a profound influence on consumer behaviour in the contemporary digital era. Organisations have the ability to employ digital marketing tactics in order to effectively reach their intended audience and harness the potential of social media platforms to cultivate brand recognition and shape consumer purchasing behaviours. A comprehensive comprehension of consumer purchasing behaviour is imperative for businesses seeking to formulate efficacious marketing strategies that resonate with their intended audience. Through obtaining a comprehensive understanding of the preferences, needs, and motivations of their clientele, enterprises can effectively devise and deliver products and services that align with their requirements and anticipations, thereby fostering increased sales and facilitating business expansion.

1. FACTORS INFLUENCING CONSUMER BUYING BEHAVIOR

Consumer purchasing behaviour is impacted by a multitude of factors that can be broadly classified into four distinct categories:

1. **Psychological factors** : encompass an individual's motivations, attitudes, beliefs, and perceptions. The subjective evaluation of a product or service by an individual can significantly impact their inclination to make a purchase. For instance, individuals who hold the belief that a specific product possesses superior quality are inclined to exhibit a higher propensity to engage in its purchase.
2. **Social factors**: encompass the impact of familial, peer, and reference group dynamics on the decision-making process of individuals when it comes to purchasing. An individual may choose to acquire a product based on its popularity within their social circle or upon receiving a recommendation from a family member or friend.
3. **Cultural factors** : encompass the influence of cultural values, norms, and beliefs on the purchasing decisions made by individuals. Consumer behaviour can be significantly influenced by the diverse values and beliefs prevalent in various cultures. In certain cultural contexts, the act of acquiring luxury goods is perceived as indicative of prosperity and affluence.
4. **Personal factors** : encompass various individual characteristics, including but not limited to age, gender, income, and lifestyle. For instance, the income level of an individual can significantly impact their consumer behaviour. Individuals with a comparatively higher income tend to exhibit a greater propensity to acquire luxury goods, whereas individuals with a relatively lower income tend to prioritise affordability in their purchasing decisions.

Additional variables that may exert an impact on consumer purchasing behaviour encompass the marketing mix, which comprises elements such as product, price, promotion, and place. Furthermore, situational factors, including temporal considerations such as the time of day or year, as well as external factors like economic circumstances, technological progressions, and political occurrences, can also play a significant role.

Gaining a comprehensive understanding of these factors and their impact on consumer behaviour is imperative for businesses seeking to formulate efficacious marketing strategies that resonate with their intended audience. By acquiring a comprehensive understanding of the preferences, requirements, and underlying motivations of their clientele, enterprises can effectively formulate and deliver offerings that align with their demands and anticipations, thereby stimulating sales and fostering organisational expansion.

2. THE CONSUMER DECISION-MAKING PROCESS

The Consumer Decision-Making Process refers to the sequential steps that individuals undertake in order to make choices, acquire, utilise, and ultimately discard goods and services with the intention of fulfilling their desires and requirements. The purchase decision-making process is characterised by a five-stage framework that consumers typically undergo. The aforementioned stages include:

1. **Problem Identification**: The initial phase of the consumer decision-making process entails the recognition of a need for a particular product or service. This phenomenon can occur as a result of either internal or external stimuli. An illustration of internal stimuli encompasses the physiological needs of a consumer, such as hunger, thirst, or the inclination for entertainment. External stimuli encompass a range of factors, including advertising, recommendations from acquaintances, and needs that emerge as a result of alterations in one's life circumstances.

2. **Information Search**: The process of information search commences once consumers have identified a need and subsequently embark on seeking relevant information pertaining to products or services that have the potential to fulfil said need. The acquisition of this information can stem from diverse sources, including personal encounters, promotional materials, endorsements from acquaintances and relatives, or evaluations found on the internet.

3. **Evaluation of Alternatives** : Following the acquisition of information regarding prospective products or services, consumers initiate the process of evaluating their available choices. Individuals engage in a comparative analysis of various alternatives, evaluating their respective attributes, advantages, and financial implications in order to ascertain the most suitable option that aligns with their requirements.

4. **Purchase Decision:** Following a thorough evaluation of available alternatives, consumers arrive at a final determination regarding their purchase. Consumers have the option to either make an immediate purchase of the product or service, or to postpone their decision for additional contemplation.

5. **Post-purchase evaluation** is the subsequent stage wherein consumers assess their experience with a particular product or service subsequent to making a purchase. Individuals may experience either a sense of satisfaction or dissatisfaction depending on their expectations and personal encounters. Customers who express satisfaction are more inclined to engage in repeat purchases and provide positive recommendations for the product or service to others. In the event of dissatisfaction, individuals have the option to engage in several actions, including returning the product or service, lodging a complaint with the company, or disseminating their negative encounter to others.

3. THE BLACK BOX MODEL

The Black Box Model serves as a conceptual framework employed to elucidate the intricacies of the consumer decision-making process. The process is metaphorically depicted as a "black box," wherein inputs are introduced and outputs are generated, yet the internal mechanisms remain concealed or incompletely comprehended. The utilisation of this model is prevalent in the field of marketing research and advertising, primarily for the purpose of examining and analysing consumer behaviour.

As depicted in the aforementioned figure, the external stimuli that elicit responses from consumers encompass the marketing mix as well as various environmental factors within the market. The marketing mix, commonly referred to as the four Ps, encompasses a collection of planned and developed stimuli devised by the organisation. The environmental stimuli are derived from the economic, political, and cultural factors that shape a society. Collectively, these factors encompass external circumstances that contribute to the formation of consumer choices.

The phenomenon of internal factors influencing consumer decisions is commonly referred to as the "black box." This conceptual construct encompasses a multitude of factors that reside within an individual's cognitive realm. These encompass various attributes of the consumer, such as their beliefs, values, motivation, lifestyle, and other related factors. The decision-making process is an integral component of the black box, wherein consumers acknowledge the existence of a problem and deliberate on how a purchasing decision can potentially address the problem. The consumer, in response to external stimuli, engages in a decision-making process influenced by internal factors, which ultimately determines their response, namely whether or not to make a purchase.

Similar to the economic man model, this particular model also posits that the consumer's response is a product of a deliberate and rational decision-making process, regardless of the internal workings of the consumer's mind, which are metaphorically referred to as the "black box." There exists a degree of scepticism among marketers regarding this assumption, as they contend that consumers frequently succumb to irrational or emotionally-driven purchasing choices. Marketers possess an understanding that the susceptibility of consumers to marketing stimuli is frequently attributed to their irrationality and emotional tendencies.

Due to this rationale, the phenomenon of consumer purchasing behaviour is widely regarded as an enigmatic or opaque entity. When individuals lack a comprehensive understanding of the underlying factors influencing their decision-making, the process of exchange becomes unpredictable and poses challenges for marketers seeking to comprehend it.

CHAPTER IV

ANALYSIS AND INTERPRETATION

TABLE 4.1

NORMALITY AND COLLINEARITY TEST RESULTS BY ITEM WISE OF DIMENSIONS INFLUENCING PURCHASE INTENTION OF GI PRODUCTS

Item Label	Normality test		Collinearity & Autocorrelation Statistics			
	Skewness	Kurtosis	Tolerance	VIF	Condition Indices	Durbin-Watson Statistic
Economic Factor (GI_EF)						
GI_EF_1	0.926	0.413	0.578	1.730	6.542	
GI_EF_2	0.597	-0.118	0.606	1.649	7.620	
GI_EF_3	0.858	-0.039	0.544	1.837	7.836	1.875
GI_EF_4	0.959	0.176	0.513	1.949	8.266	
GI_EF_5	0.959	0.319	.471	2.123	8.827	
Socio-cultural Factor (GI_SCEF)						
GI_SCEF_1	1.057	0.453	0.398	2.512	6.452	
GI_SCEF_2	0.967	0.174	0.398	2.516	7.339	
GI_SCEF_3	0.594	-0.622	0.664	1.507	7.724	1.914
GI_SCEF_4	1.065	0.422	0.538	1.859	7.836	
GI_SCEF_5	0.824	-0.048	0.602	1.660	8.456	
GI_SCEF_6	0.738	-0.019	0.583	1.716	10.523	
Psychological Factor (GI_PSYF)						
GI_PSYF_1	0.782	-0.161	0.561	1.781	5.836	
GI_PSYF_2	0.752	-0.332	0.650	1.539	7.023	
GI_PSYF_3	0.994	0.198	0.270	3.710	7.527	1.959
GI_PSYF_4	1.084	0.430	0.272	3.683	7.807	
GI_PSYF_5	0.684	-0.250	0.573	1.745	12.418	
Personal Factor (GI_PERF)						
GI_PERF_1	0.164	-0.998	0.516	1.937	6.175	
GI_PERF_2	0.618	-0.621	0.506	1.977	7.715	1.948
GI_PERF_3	0.581	-0.687	0.503	1.988	8.007	
GI_PERF_4	0.401	-0.807	0.541	1.847	8.577	
Purchase Intention (PUR_INT)						
PUR_INT_1	0.971	-0.049	0.216	4.626	5.344	
PUR_INT_2	0.988	0.053	0.227	4.407	6.882	1.994
PUR_INT_3	0.795	-0.092	0.539	1.854	7.407	
PUR_INT_4	0.851	-0.207	0.554	1.804	12.283	

Normal univariate distribution (George & Mallery, 2010). George, D., & Mallery, M. (2010).

Normality and Collinearity

The ***Normality holds as the values are within the specified range of skewness and Kurtosis for all the items (Table 13).*** Hence the assumption of normality holds for item under each dimension influencing PURCHASE INTENTION of buying GI products. Furthermore, the Variance Inflation 'Factor (VIF) of all the items is below the recommend value of 5 and also tolerance value less than 1. This indicates that there is very less collinearity and there is no possibility of inflated variance of the items. Furthermore, with regard to *autocorrelation*, Durbin Watson statistics is calculated. A **rule of thumb** is that test statistic values in the range of 1.5 to 2.5 are relatively normal & outside of this range could be cause for concern. Field (2009). In the table above, the Durbin Watson statistics for all dimensions is within the acceptable value and can proceed for CFA and SEM analysis.

EXHIBIT 4.1

MEASUREMENT MODEL OF DIMENSIONS INFLUENCING PURCHASE INTENTION WITH STANDARD REGRESSION ESTIMATES

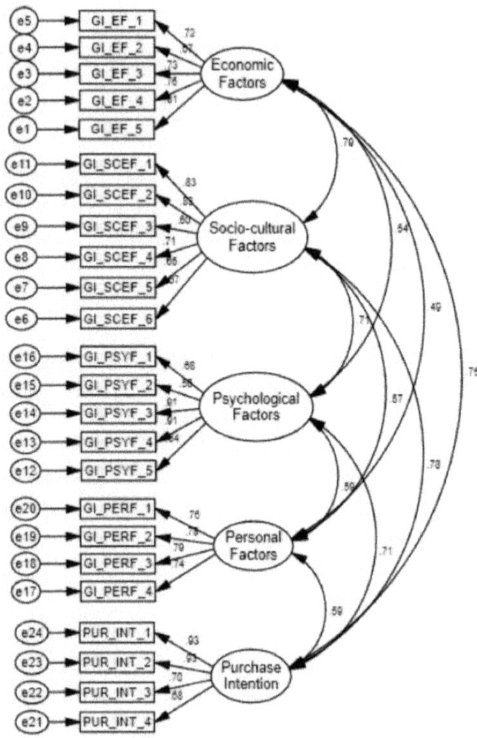

Measurement Model of Dimension

4.1 AUTOCORRELATION TEST

Autocorrelation test is to determine the correlation between disorders that are no longer efficient to estimators in small samples or models with large samples. The presence of autocorrelation can be detect by using Durbin- Watson test (DW). The result is then will be compared with F table. When the result of DW is smaller than F table (DW < F table), then there is no autocorrelation in the regression and vice versa.

TABLE 4.2

CORRELATION (COVARIANCE) RESULT OF DIMENSIONS INFLUENCING PURCHASE INTENTION OF GI PRODUCTS

Dimension	Correlation value				
	GI_EF	GI_SCEF	GI_PSYF	GI_PERF	PUR_INT
GI_EF	-	0.793	0.540	0.488	0.710
GI_SCEF	-	-	0.570	0.588	0.751
GI_PSYF	-	-	-	0.783	0.705
GI_PERF	-	-	-	-	0.589

Table 4.3 shows the inter item Correlation (Covariance) result of dimensions of dimensions influencing Purchase Intention of GI products for Full-fledged data. Accordingly, it is observed that there is a good correlation between any two given dimensions.

Auto Correlation

4.2 GOODNESS-OF-FIT

Goodness-of-fit refers to a statistical test that determines how well sample data fits a distribution from a population with a normal distribution. Put simply, it hypothesizes whether a sample is skewed or represents the data you would expect to find in the actual population.

TABLE 4.3

GOODNESS-OF-FIT & INCREMENTAL INDICES OF MEASUREMENT MODEL FOR DIMENSIONS INFLUENCING PURCHASE INTENTION OF GI PRODUCTS

	(χ^2/df)	GFI	RMSEA	AGFI	NFI	CFI	IFI	RFI	PCFI	PNFI
Accepted Value	< 5	> 0.90	< 0.10	> 0.80	> 0.90				> 0.50	
Model Value	2.994	0.873	0.059	0.843	0.915	0.942	0.942	0.903	0.826	0.802

Table 4.4 depict the Goodness-of-fit & Incremental Indices of Measurement model for Full-fledged data for dimensions influencing Purchase Intention of GI products. The model shows an overall acceptable fit and is an over identified model and hence proceed for SEM analysis.

Goodness of fit

 SOCIO ECONOMIC PROFILE OF THE RESPONDENTS

TABLE 4.4

GENDER REPRESENTATION

Gender	Frequency	Percent
Male	282	49.9
Female	283	50.1
Total	565	100.0

EXHIBIT 4.2

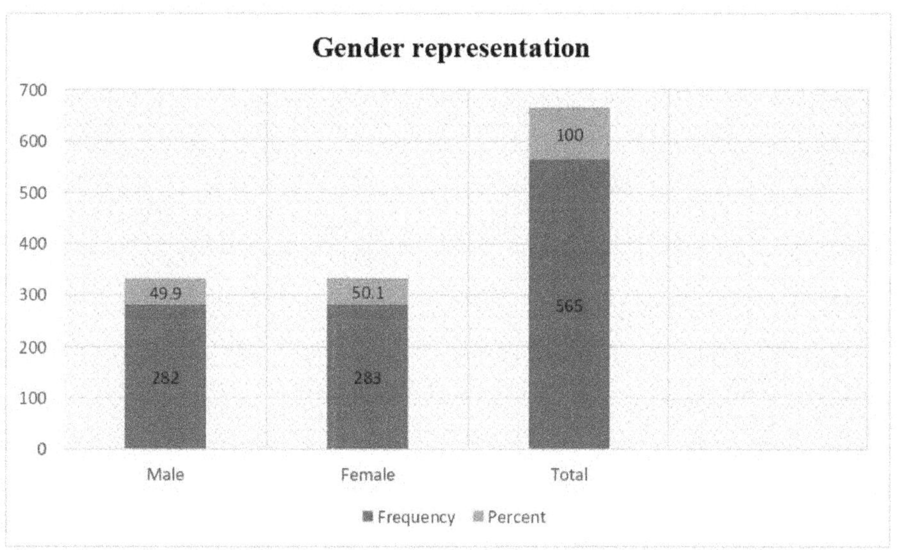

The gender of the consumers depicts that female respondents are slightly higher than male. This indicates the segment of target GI Consumers.

Gender

TABLE 4.5

AGE GROUP OF THE RESPONDENTS

Age (Yrs.)	Frequency	Percent
< 30	134	23.7
30-40	225	39.8
40-50	120	21.2
50 and above	86	15.2
Total	565	100.0

EXHIBIT 4.3

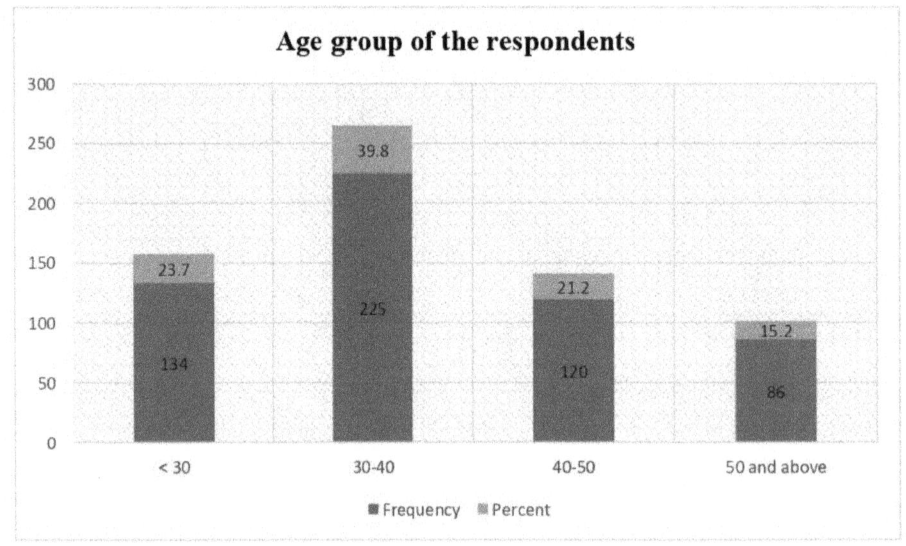

In terms of age, 23.7 per cent of respondents are under 30 years old, while 39.8 per cent are between 30 and 40 years old. Similarly, 21.2 per cent of them are between the ages of 40 and 50, with 15.2 per cent being over the age of 50.

Age

TABLE 4.6

TYPE OF THE FAMILY

Family Type	Frequency	Percent
Nuclear	383	67.8
Joint	182	32.2
Total	565	100.0

EXHIBIT 4.4

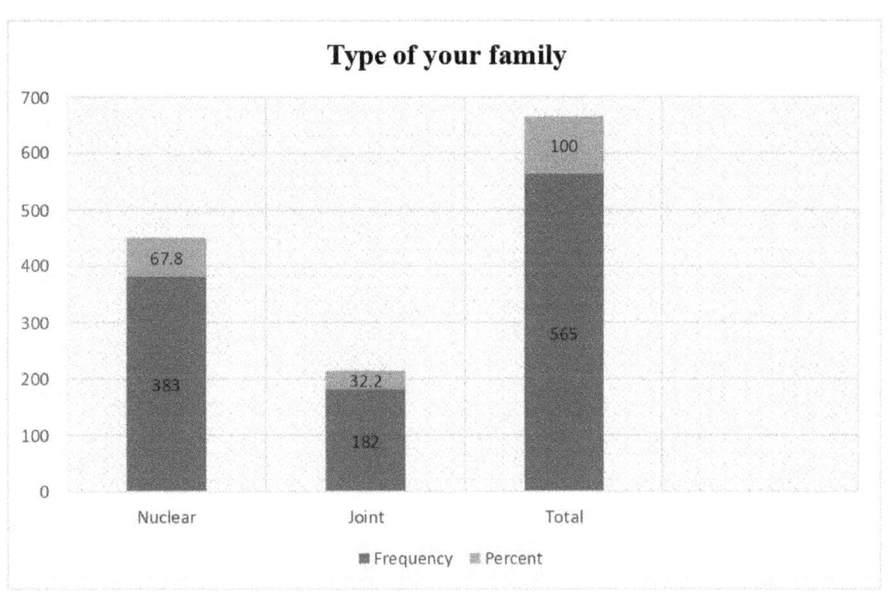

Regarding the type of family majority of the respondents (67.8 percent) respondents are living in nuclear family and 32.2 percent from joint family.

Family

TABLE 4.7

EDUCATION QUALIFICATION OF RESPONDENTS

Qualification	Frequency	Percent
Primary	73	12.9
High School	132	23.4
Graduate	218	38.6
Post Graduate	90	15.9
Professional	52	9.2
Total	565	100.0

EXHIBIT 4.5

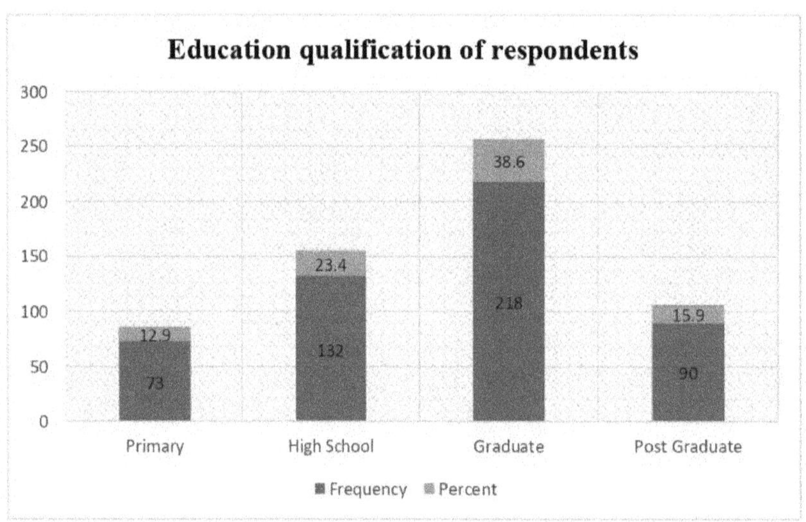

In terms of education, most of the consumers are having graduation or above qualification, and 23.4 percent completed their high schooling and 9.2 percent are professionals.

Qualification

TABLE 4.8 NATURE

OF OCCUPATION

Occupation	Frequency	Percent
Student	39	6.9
Private sector	236	41.8
Govt sector	165	29.2
Business	86	15.2
Home maker	26	4.6
Self Employed	13	2.3
Total	565	100.0

EXHIBIT 4.6

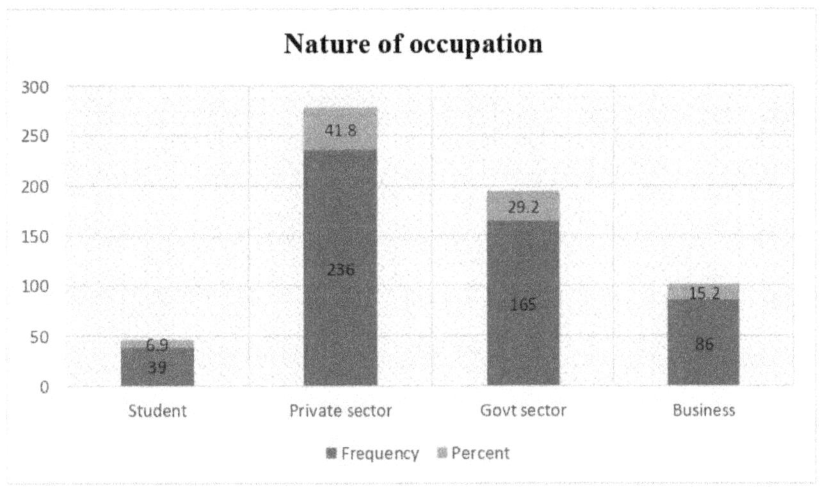

In terms of occupational status, it is observed that more than one-fourth (29.2 per cent) of respondents are working in Govt. sector, 41.8 per cent are employed in private sector, and the remaining 15.2 per cent have been successful in running their own business. Perhaps, occupational status could also be considered as another indicator for analysis of the consumers' likelihood of purchase of GI Products.

Occupation

TABLE 4.9

MONTHLY INCOME OF THE FAMILY

Income	Frequency	Percent
< Rs 10,000	80	14.2
10,000-20,000	135	23.9
20,000-30,000	269	47.6
> Rs 30,000	81	14.3
Total	565	100.0

EXHIBIT 4.7

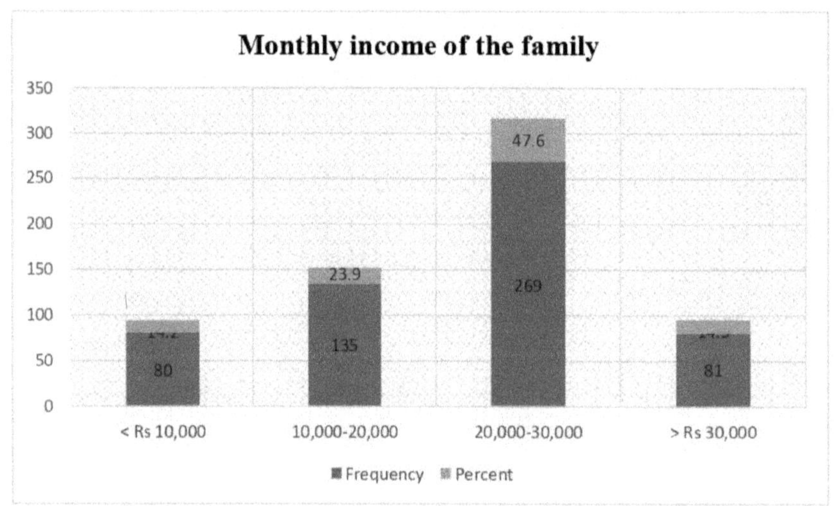

It also shows that nearly half (47.6 per cent) of survey participants have monthly income between 20000-30000, while nearby one four (23.9 per cent) have monthly household income between 10000-20000. It is a known fact that household income is a key determinant in analysing consumers' consumption behaviour and it is evident that GI Tagged products are affordable for the consumers like all other normal category of goods.

Income

TABLE 4.10

FREQUENCY OF BUYING GI PRODCTS

Buying Frequency	Frequency	Percent
Daily	39	6.9
Weekly	59	10.4
Monthly	176	31.2
As required	291	51.5
Total	565	100.0

EXHIBIT 4.8

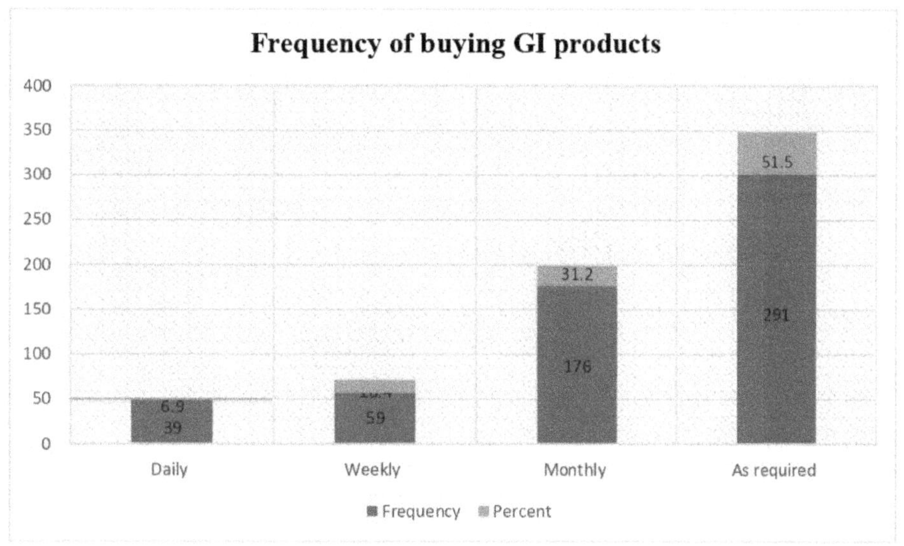

Regarding the frequency of purchase of GI products more than half (51.5 per cent) of respondents purchased the product when required nor based on the demand. Correspondingly, roughly 31 per cent of interviewees indicated that they would buy monthly Remarkably, 10.5 per cent of them buy GI products weekly. This indicates the adequate demand of the GI Tagged products among the buyers.

Frequency

TABLE 4.11 LOCALITY

OF RESPONDENTS

District	Frequency	Percent
Palakkad	264	46.8
Alappuzha	222	39.2
Wayanad	79	14.0
Total	565	100.0

EXHIBIT 4.9

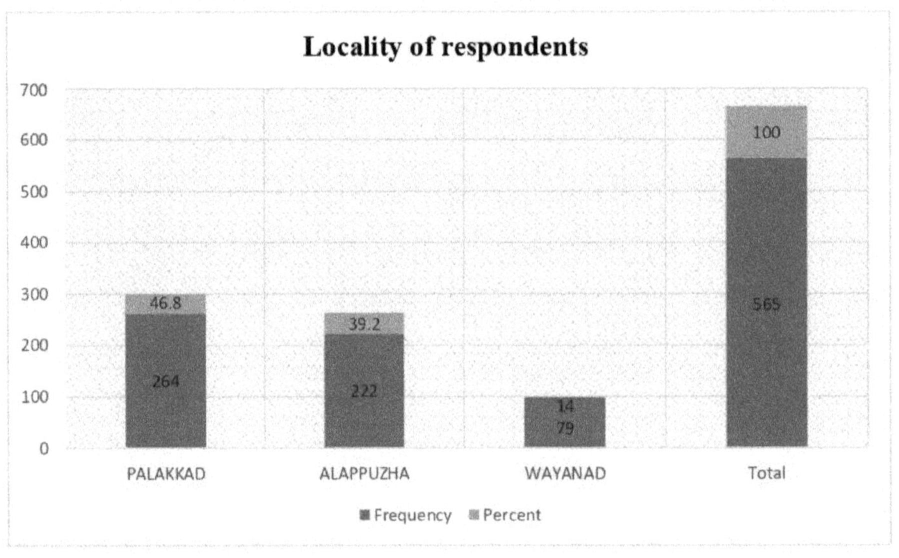

Regarding the locality of respondents 46.8 percent are from Palakkad, 39.2 percent from Alappuzha, and remaining 14 percent are from Wayanad.

Locality

4.4 LEVEL OF WARENESS OF THE RESPONDENTS TOWARDS GI PRODUCTS

TABLE 4.12

RESPONDENTS AWARENESS ON GI TAG/LABEL

Awareness	Frequency	Per cent
Highly aware	227	26.0
Less aware	274	55.5
Not Aware at all	64	18.5
Total	565	100.0

EXHIBIT 4.10

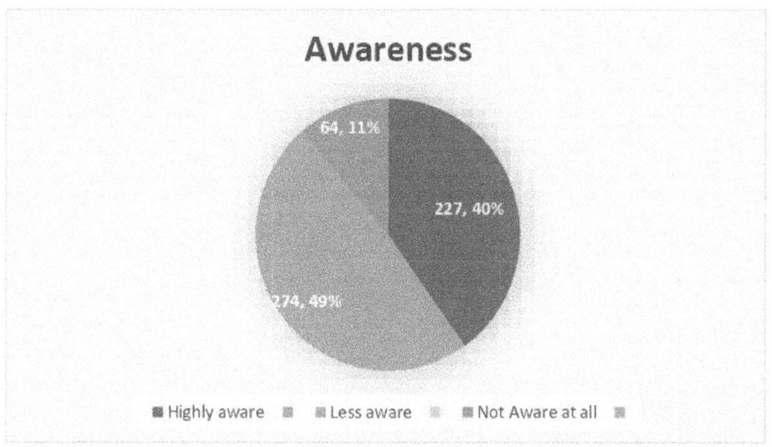

The awareness of GI Tag is very less among the consumers. The purchasing is done based on the product name rather than the tag. There is a need to bring huge awareness of GI Tag and the benefits of the product to the consumers. Only by intensive promotion the awareness of the tag can be increased.

Awareness

TABLE 4.13

AWARENESS TOWARDS GI PRODUCTS OF KERALA

Sl.No	Product	Percentage of Respondents				
		Well Aware	Aware	Moderate	Not Aware	Not All Aware
1.	Aranmulla Kannadi	49.9	35.2	11.2	3.7	-
2.	Alleppey Coir	20.4	18.9	20.7	31.2	8.8
3.	Maddalam of Palakkad	47.8	28.5	9.9	11.5	2.3
4.	Screw Pine Craft of Kerala	7.4	20.4	27.8	34.0	10.4
5.	Brass Broidered Coconut Shell Crafts of Kerala	8.1	18.8	28.0	33.1	12.0
6.	Payyannur Pavithra Ring	8.1	18.8	28.0	33.1	12.0
7.	Cannanore Home Furnishings	7.4	20.4	27.8	34.0	10.4
8.	Balaramapuram Sarees and Fine Cotton Fabrics	34.0	37.0	22.7	3.2	3.2
9.	Kasargod Sarees	46.7	37.7	12.0	3.5	-
10.	Kuthampully Sarees on Fine Cotton	47.8	28.5	9.9	11.5	2.3
11.	Chendamangalam Dhoties & Set Mundu	44.6	34.2	17.7	1.8	1.8
12.	Kuthampally Dhoties & Set Mundu	47.8	28.5	9.9	11.5	2.3
13.	Navara Rice	34.0	37.0	22.7	3.2	3.2
14.	Palakkadan Matta Rice	58.4	32.6	4.4	4.6	-
15.	Pokkali Rice	8.3	18.8	27.8	33.1	12.0
16.	Vazhakulam Pineapple	37.5	39.5	18.8	4.2	-
17.	Kaipad Rice	7.4	20.4	27.8	34.0	10.4
18.	Chengalikodan Nendran Banana	26.2	27.6	20.2	19.6	6.4
19.	Tirur Betel Leaf	8.1	18.8	28.0	33.1	12.0

Sl.No	Product	Percentage of Respondents				
		Well Aware	Aware	Moderate	Not Aware	Not All Aware
20.	Malabar Pepper	47.8	35.2	4.6	9.9	2.5
21.	Monsooned Malabar Robusta Coffee	34.0	37.0	22.7	3.2	3.2
22.	Alleppey Green Cardamom	27.6	28.0	20.0	18.1	6.4
23.	Wayanad Jeerakasala Rice	43.0	38.2	12.4	6.4	-
24.	Wayanad Robusta Coffee	46.7	37.7	12.0	3.5	-
25.	Wayanad Gandhakasala Rice	46.0	37.3	12.0	4.6	-
26.	Central Travancore Jaggery	36.5	32.7	16.1	11.5	3.2
27.	Marayoor Jaggery	51.2	38.2	8.0	2.7	-
28.	Nilambur Teak	51.2	37.9	8.3	2.7	-

Regarding awareness of respondents towards Geographical Indication products, 58.4 per cent respondents are well aware about Palakkadan matta rice, Almost Half of the Respondents well aware about Marayoor Jaggery and Nilabur teak i.e., 53.07 per cent of the Respondnts. Aranmulla Kannadi is the Fourth Popular Product among the GI Products of Kerala. About 47.8 percent respondents well aware about Kuthampullly dhoties and Maddalam of Palakkad. 34 per cent respondents not aware about Cannanore home furnishings. Brass Broidered Coconut Shell Crafts of Kerala, Payyannur Pavithra Ring, Tirur Betel Leaf are the least known GI Product of Kerala among respondents Respondents having well awareness towards More than 90 per cent of the Geographical products of Kerala.

Even though consumers are familiar with the majority of products labelled with a geographical indication, consumers do not know very much about products such as Screw Pine Craft of Kerala, Tirur Betel Leaf, Cannanore Home Furnishings, Pokkali Rice, etc. As a result, producers and the government should take the necessary steps to raise awareness of the products and promote them among consumers. Only then will these products be able to reach consumers.

Products

4.6 PURCHASE PATTERN OF RESPONDENTS TOWARDS GI PRODUCTS

TABLE 4.14

GI TAGGED PRODUCTS OF KERALA AND THE PURCHASING PATTERN OF THE RESPONDENTS

No	Product	Percent
1.	Aranmulla Kannadi	16.6
2.	Alleppey Coir	4.7
3.	Maddalam of Palakkad	0.5
4.	Screw Pine Craft of Kerala	0.9
5.	Brass Broidered Coconut Shell Crafts of Kerala	1.2
6.	Payyannur Pavithra Ring	2.3
7.	Cannanore Home Furnishings	1.8
8.	Balaramapuram Sarees and Fine Cotton Fabrics	4.8
9.	Kasargod Sarees	3.2
10.	Kuthampully Sarees on Fine Cotton	28.2
11.	Chendamangalam Dhoties & Set Mundu	6.5
12.	Kuthampally Dhoties & Set Mundu	10.1
13.	Navara Rice	11.2
14.	Palakkadan Matta Rice	24.3
15.	Pokkali Rice	8.2
16.	Vazhakulam Pineapple	6.5
17.	Kaipad Rice	4.5
18.	Chengalikodan Nendran Banana	5.0
19.	Tirur Betel Leaf	1.7

GI Products of Kerala

No	Product	Percent
20.	Malabar Pepper	21.4
21.	Monsooned Malabar Robusta Coffee	7.9
22.	Alleppey Green Cardamom	5.8
23.	Wayanad Jeerakasala Rice	10.6
24.	Wayanad Robusta Coffee	6.5
25.	Wayanad Gandhakasala Rice	12.6
26.	Central Travancore Jaggery	5.8
27.	Marayoor Jaggery	14.5
28.	Nilambur Teak	3.1

Regarding GI product consumption, respondents were given an exhaustive list of GI products manufactured in Kerala. The respondents were asked to opt from the products that they regularly purchase. Accordingly, Kuthampully Sarees (28.2 per cent) are the most popular GI products among respondents, followed by Palakkadan Matta Rice (24.3 per cent), Malabar Pepper (21.4) Aranmula Kannadi (22.6 per cent), Kuthampully Set Mundu (20.3 per cent), and. (19.0). This appears to be evident given that the four topmost GI products are purchased by a more significant segment of the consumer society for auspicious occasions such as marriages, festivals, and other important social events. The other GI products that are exclusively bought are Malabar Pepper (17.0 per cent), Kuthampully Dhoties (14.7 per cent) and Balarampuram saree and fine cotton Fabrics (13.7 per cent).

GI Products of Kerala

TABLE 4.15

PREFERENCE AMONG THE RESPONDENTS TO BUY GI TAGGED PRODUCTS

Purchase Preference	Frequency	Per cent
Always offline	110	19.5
Always Online	136	24.1
Both (Depends on the availability of the product)	319	56.4
Total	565	100.0

EXHIBIT 4.11

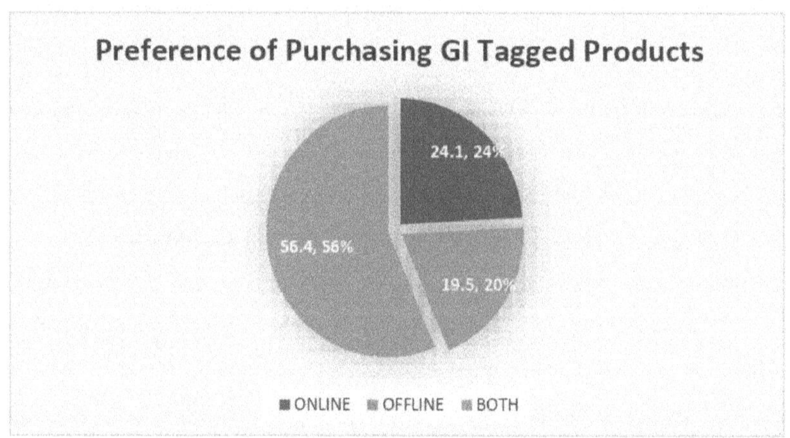

Regarding preference to buy GI Products online or offline, the consumers revealed that only 19.5 per cent of respondents always prefer to buy offline. In contrast, slightly more than one-fourth (24.1 per cent) always prefer to buy online (digital). Nonetheless, it is clear that more than half of them prefer both online and offline purchases based on price and other discounts.

Preference

4.7 FACTORS INFLUENCING CONSUMER BUYING BEHAVIOR OF GEOGRAPHICAL INDICATION PRODUCTS

SEM ANALYSIS RESULT

In present context of our SEM model results, we first look at the direct relationship between each of the independent dimension with the dependent dimension as below.

H₁: ECONOMIC FACTOR HAS A SIGNIFICANT INFLUENCE/IMPACT ON PURCHASE INTENTION OF RESPONDENTS TOWARDS BUYING OF GI PRODUCTS.

The above hypothesis is addressed using zero order correlation SEM technique. The relationship between *Economic factor* and *Purchase Intention* is depicted in exhibit 4.12.

EXHIBIT 4.12

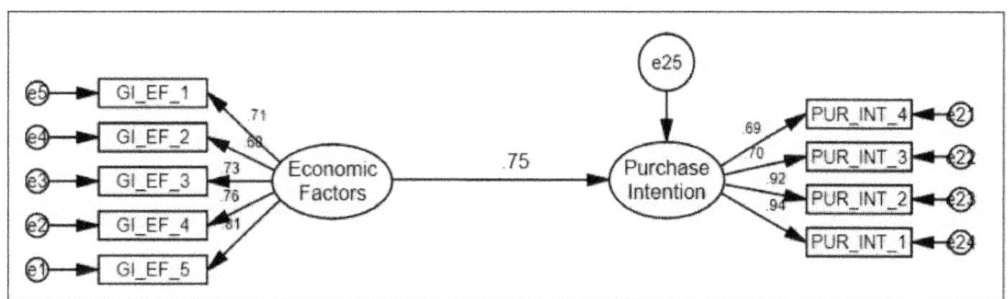

Relationship between *Economic factor* and *Purchase Intention*

TABLE 4.16

STANDARDIZED REGRESSION WEIGHTS FOR DIRECT RELATIONSHIP BETWEEN ECONOMIC FACTOR AND PURCHASE INTENTION

			Standard Estimate	S.E.	C.R.	P
Purchase Intention	<---	*Economic factor*	0.752	0.052	14.029	0.000*

* Significant at 5% level.

Economic factor and Purchase Intention

The regression result is provided in Table. Accordingly, it is observed that *Economic factor* has a significant (ß = 0.752; CR = 14.029, p<0.05) influence/impact on *Purchase Intention of GI products*, thus, H₁ could be fully asserted. The interpretation is that, for one unit increase in the rating scale of agreement on *Economic factor* construct, one could expect about 0.752 times (about 75 %) increase in the agreement towards *Purchase Intention* given other factors remain fixed or same. In other words, for every new 10 respondents rating as agree or strongly agree for *Economic factor* dimension, one would expect about **seven** respondents (ß = 0.752) likely to give a rating of agree or strongly agree on *Purchase Intention* dimension.

Economic factors such as Family income, Willingness to pay, and Superior products at competitive price, having a greater impact on Purchase intentions of consumers towards buying of Geographical Indication Products. So these economic aspects of the Geographical Indication products should be considered by the producers and marketers then only the successful market segmentation and market expansion strategies will be successful.

H₂: SOCIO-CULTURAL FACTOR HAS A SIGNIFICANT INFLUENCE/IMPACT ON PURCHASE INTENTION OF RESPONDENTS TOWARDS BUYING OF GI PRODUCTS.

EXHIBIT 4.13

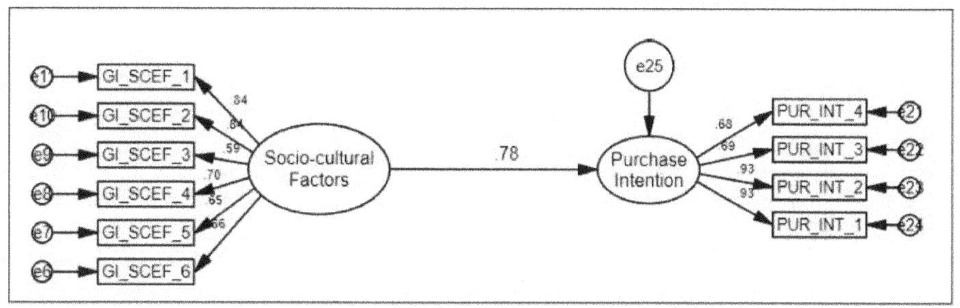

Relationship between *Socio-cultural factor* and *Purchase Intention*

TABLE 4.17

STANDARDIZED REGRESSION WEIGHTS FOR DIRECT RELATIONSHIP BETWEEN SOCIO-CULTURAL FACTOR AND PURCHASE INTENTION

			Standard Estimate	S.E.	C.R.	P
Purchase Intention	<---	*Socio-cultural factor*	0.782	0.070	12.652	0.000*

* Significant at 5% level.

The regression result is provided in Table 4.18 & Figure 4.13. Accordingly, it is observed that *Socio-cultural factor* has a significant (ß = 0.782; CR = 12.652, p<0.05) influence/impact on *Purchase Intention of GI products*, thus, H₂ could be fully asserted. The interpretation is that, for one unit increase in the rating scale of agreement on *Socio-cultural factor* construct, one could expect about 0.782 times (about 78 %) increase in the agreement towards *Purchase Intention* given other factors remain fixed or same. In other words, for every new 10 respondents rating as agree or strongly agree for *Socio-cultural factor* dimension, one would expect about **eight** respondents (ß = 0.782) likely to give a rating of agree or strongly agree on *Purchase Intention* dimension.

Socio cultural factor

The various socio cultural factors like, culture and its heritage, a diverse nature of tastes, conservative beliefs, and Traditional Values and benefits significantly affects the purchase intentions of the respondents, so these socio cultural factors determines the survival and growth of geographical indication products, marketers of GI Products should study the socio cultural factors of Geographical Indication Products.

H₃: PSYCHOLOGICAL FACTOR HAS A SIGNIFICANT INFLUENCE/IMPACT ON PURCHASE INTENTION OF RESPONDENTS TOWARDS BUYING OF GI PRODUCTS.

EXHIBIT 4.14

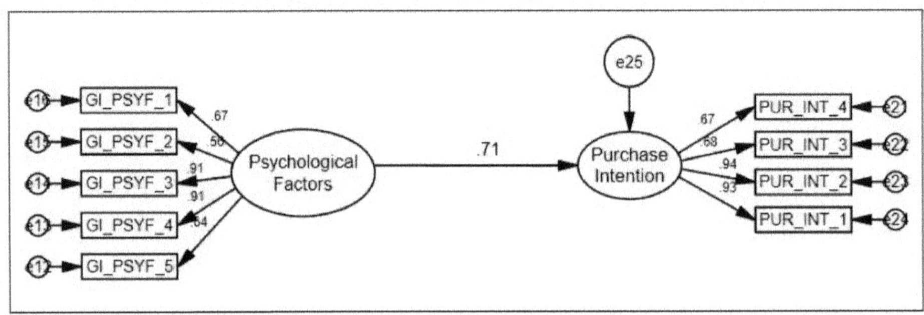

Figure 6: Relationship between *Psychological factor* and *Purchase Intention*

TABLE 4.18

STANDARDIZED REGRESSION WEIGHTS FOR DIRECT RELATIONSHIP BETWEEN PSYCHOLOGICAL FACTOR AND PURCHASE INTENTION

			Standard Estimate	S.E.	C.R.	P
Purchase Intention	<---	*Psychological factor*	0.705	0.067	11.731	0.000*

* Significant at 5% level.

The regression result is provided in Table 4.19 & Figure 4.14. Accordingly, it is observed that *Psychological factor* has a significant (ß = 0.705; CR = 11.731, p<0.05) influence/impact on *Purchase Intention of GI products*, thus, H₃ could be fully asserted.

Psychological factor

The interpretation is that, for one unit increase in the rating scale of agreement on *Psychological* construct, one could expect about 0.705 times (about 70 %) increase in the agreement towards *Purchase Intention* given other factors remain fixed or same. In other words, for every new 10 respondents rating as agree or strongly agree for *Psychological factor* dimension, one would expect about **seven** respondents (ß = 0.705) likely to give a rating of agree or strongly agree on *Purchase Intention* dimension.

H$_4$: PERSONAL FACTOR HAS A SIGNIFICANT INFLUENCE/IMPACT ON PURCHASE INTENTION OF RESPONDENTS TOWARDS BUYING OF GI PRODUCTS.

EXHIBIT 4.15

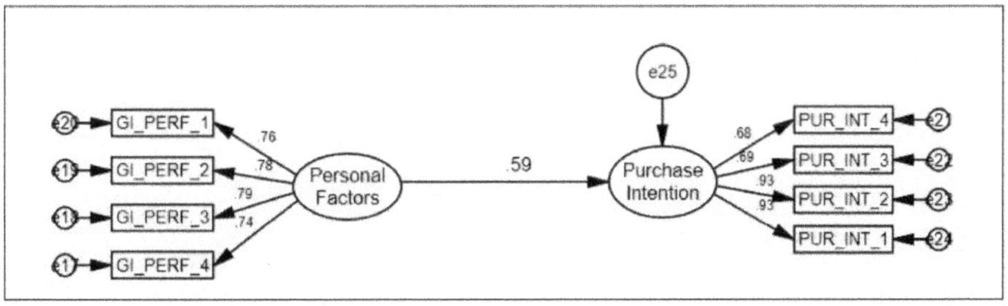

Relationship between *Personal factor* and *Purchase Intention*

TABLE 4.19

STANDARDIZED REGRESSION WEIGHTS FOR DIRECT RELATIONSHIP BETWEEN PERSONAL AND PURCHASE INTENTION

			Standard Estimate	S.E.	C.R.	P
Purchase Intention	<---	*Personal factor*	0.573	0.052	10.991	0.000*

* Significant at 5% level.

The regression result is provided in Table 4.20 & Figure 4.15. Accordingly, it is observed that *Personal factor* has a significant (ß = 0.573; CR = 10.991, p<0.05) influence/impact on *Purchase Intention of GI products*, thus, H$_4$ could be fully asserted. The interpretation is that, for one unit increase in the rating scale of agreement on *Personal*

Personal Factors

construct, one could expect about 0.573 times (about 57%) increase in the agreement towards *Purchase Intention* given other factors remain fixed or same. In other words, for every new 10 respondents rating as agree or strongly agree for *Personal* dimension, one would expect about **six** respondents (ß = 0.573) likely to give a rating of agree or strongly agree on *Purchase Intention* dimension.

Various personal factors such as family, life style, social status, suitability to age and income having a greater impact on the purchase intention of consumers towards buying of GI products.

4.8 LEVEL OF SATISFACTION OF CUSTOMERS TOWARDS GEOGRAPHICAL INDICATION PRODUCTS

TABLE 4.20

PERCENTAGE OF RESPONDENTS ACROSS EACH SATISFACTION INDICATOR OF POST PURCHASE OF GI PRODUCTS

		Percentage (in %) of Respondents				
	Satisfaction Indicator	**HS (1)**	**S (2)**	**N(3)**	**D (4)**	**HD(5)**
1	*Quality* of the product	54.2	41.2	3.0	1.6	0.0
2	*Durability* of the product	52.6	38.6	8.8	0.0	0.0
3	*Usefulness* of the product	52.9	38.2	8.8	0.0	0.0
4	*Price* of the product	15.4	50.3	32.7	1.6	0.0
5	*Design* of the product	60.9	36.5	2.7	0.0	0.0
6	*Eco friendly* features	64.6	32.2	3.2	0.0	0.0
7	Worth for money	50.8	42.8	6.4	0.0	0.0
8	Nature and features of the product	58.4	35.4	6.2	0.0	0.0
9	*Packing* of the product	9.4	22.5	39.8	25.8	2.5
10	Availability of the product	5.1	19.3	31.5	29.0	15.0
11.	After Sale Issues	7.8	22.7	34.9	27.6	7.1
12.	Pride of Possession	64.6	32.0	3.4	0.0	0.0

Note: HS – Highly Satisfied; S – Satisfied; N – Neutral; D-Dissatisfied; HD – Highly Dissatisfied

111

Post Purchase

Consumers are highly satisfied with Design, Pride of possession and eco friendly features of geographical indication products 64.6 per cent and 60.9 per cent respectively, more than half of respondents are highly satisfied with the quality, durability, usefulness and nature of the product, consumers are concerned about the packing, availability and after sale issues of the Geographical Indication products. 32.7 percent respondents have neutral opinion towards pricing of Geographical Indication Products.

TABLE 4.21

WEIGHTED AVERAGE SCORE BASED ON RANKING OF VARIOUS SATISFACTION INDICATORS BY THE RESPONDENTS IN POST PURCHASE OF GI PRODUCTS

	No. of Respondents with rank					Total	WAS*	Rank #
	#1	#2	#3	#4	#5			
Quality of the product	306	233	17	9	0.0	565	4.48	4
Durability of the product	297	218	50	0	0	565	4.44	5
Usefulness of the product	299	216	50	0	0	565	4.44	5
Price of the product	87	284	185	9	0	565	3.79	6
Design of the product	344	206	15	0	0	565	4.58	2
Eco friendly features	365	182	18	0	0	565	4.61	1
Worth for money	287	242	36	0	0	565	4.44	5
Nature and features of the product	330	200	35	0	0	565	4.52	3
Packaging of the product	53	127	225	146	14	565	3.10	7
Availability of the product	29	109	178	164	85	565	2.70	9
After Sale Issues	44	128	197	156	40	565	2.96	8
Pride of possession	365	181	19	0	0	565	4.61	1

* Weighted Average Score

111

Ranking of post purchase Behavior

In this regard, the query was related to customer satisfaction in post purchase of GI products. They were asked to rank in the order of their preferences. Accordingly, it is observed from Table 4.22 that *Pride of possession and **Eco friendly** features of GI products are ranked as the first (with a WAS of 4.61)* followed by Design of the product (WAS = 4.58) as their second priority (in terms of ranking their preference) and then Nature and features of the product (WAS = 4.52) as their priority of buying GI products.

On the flip side, the lower ranking is observed with respect to ***Availability of the product*** (WAS = 2.70), After Sale Matters (WAS = 2.96) and ***Packing of the Product*** (WAS = 2.70) as their least preferred (in terms of ranking their preference) while purchase of GI products. Hence, it is suggested that the manufacturers of GI products should give more importance or emphasis on packaging of the material, to provide good customer services after purchase of GI product as well as ensure that adequate stock of the products are maintained to supply the need of the customers.

4.8.1 SATISFACTION LEVEL OF RESPONDENTS TOWARDS PACKAGING OF GI PRODUCTS

H$_5$: RESPONDENTS ARE SATISFIED WITH PACKAGE OF GI PRODUCTS

To test the above hypothesis Wilcoxon signed rank test is applied. The null hypothesis is that there is no change ("neutral") in the rating given by the respondents and so the hypothesized sign rank is 3. Now, the null and alternative hypotheses can be stated as follows.

H$_0$: Mean response is equal to 3 [sign = 0]

[Indicates that higher proportion of respondents are remaining neutral to the above statement]

H$_1$: Mean response is less than 3 [sign is negative]

[Indicates that higher proportion of respondents are "Agree" to the above statement]

H$_2$: Mean response is greater than 3 [sign is positive]

[Indicates that higher proportion of respondents are "Strongly Disagree" to the above statement]

112

Satisfaction

FREQUENCY DISTRIBUTION OF RESPONDENTS' SATISFACTION TOWARDS 'PACKAGE OF GI PRODUCTS'

Level of Agreement	No. of respondents	Percent
Highly Satisfied (1)	53	9.4
Satisfied (2)	127	22.5
Neutral (3)	225	39.8
Dissatisfied (4)	146	25.8
Highly Dissatisfied (5)	14	2.5
Total	565	100.0

Source: Primary Data Field Study

TABLE 4.23

ONE SAMPLE WILCOXON SIGNED RANK TEST RESULT

Wilcoxon signed- rank test			
Sign	**obs**	**Sum ranks**	**Expected**
Positive	160	60300	67235
Negative	180	74170	67235
Zero	225	25425	25425
All	565	159895	159895

Unadjusted variance - 15070104
Adjustment for ties - 430412.5
Adjustment for zeros - <u>955556.25</u>
Adjusted variance   13684405
Ho: varl = 3
      z   = -1.875
    prob > | z |= 0.0608

113

Package of GI Products

From the above one sample Wilcoxon signed rank test result (Table 4.24), it is observed that the p-value (0.068) is greater than the significant at 5 percent level. Hence, the null hypothesis (H_0) that a higher proportion of respondents are remaining neutral to the above statement is accepted and alternative (H_1) is rejected. It observed from the above table that there are almost a similar number of respondents with a negative sign (180 respondents) and number of respondents with a positive sign [160 respondents].

Now, as the number of respondents with a negative sign (i.e, 180, 31.9 %) is closer to that of positive sign rank (160, 28.3%), one would conclude a same proportion of respondents under the sample study believes that *Customers are satisfied as well not satisfied with Packaging of GI products in post purchase.* Nonetheless, it is observed from the descriptive statistics (Table 26) that *a considerable proportion* of the respondents (39.8 percent) have remained neutral to the above statement thus not able to arrive at a definite conclusion that *they are satisfied as well not satisfied with Packaging of GI products in post purchase.*

4.8.2 SATISFACTION LEVEL OF RESPONDENTS TOWARDS AVAILABILITY OF GI PRODUCTS

H_6: CUSTOMERS ARE SATISFIED WITH AVAILABILITY OF GI PRODUCTS IN POST PURCHASE.

TABLE 4.24

FREQUENCY DISTRIBUTION OF RESPONDENTS' SATISFACTION TOWARDS 'AVAILABILITY OF GI PRODUCTS'

Level of Agreement	No. of respondents	Percent
Highly Satisfied (1)	29	5.1
Satisfied (2)	109	19.3
Neutral (3)	178	31.5
Dissatisfied (4)	164	29.0
Highly Dissatisfied (5)	85	15.0
Total	565	100.0

114

Availability of GI Products

TABLE 4.25

ONE SAMPLE WILCOXON SIGNED RANK TEST RESULT

Wilcoxon signed- rank test			
Sign	**obs**	**Sum ranks**	**Expected**
Positive	249	94882.5	71982
Negative	138	49081.5	71982
Zero	178	15931	15931
All	565	159895	159895

Unadjusted variance 15070104

Adjustment for ties   -454741.13

Adjustment for zeros -473947.25

Adjusted variance   14141415

Ho: varl = 3

z   = 6.090

prob > | z |= 0.0000

From the above one sample Wilcoxon signed rank test result (Table 4.26), it is observed that the p-value (0.000) is less than the significant at 5 percent level. Hence, the null hypothesis (H_0) that a higher proportion of respondents are remaining neutral to the above statement is rejected and alternative (H_1) is accepted. Before accepting any one of the two alternative hypotheses, we need to observe the one sample Wilcoxon signed rank test result (Table K-8). Accordingly, there are a higher (249) number respondents with a positive sign as compared to number of respondents with a negative sign [138 respondents]. Now, as both "Dissatisfied" and "Highly Dissatisfied" has been given a scaling of 4 & 5, the positive sign indicate a higher proportion of respondents are showing dissatisfaction to the statement that *Customers are satisfied with Availability of GI products in post purchase.* On the contrary, the negative sign indicate that respondents have ranked towards "satisfied" and "Highly satisfied" to the above statement.

115

Signed Rank test

Now, as the number of respondents with a positive sign is higher (i.e, 249 > 138) than that of negative sign rank, one would conclude (statistically) that a higher proportion of respondents under the sample study believe that *Customers are not satisfied with Availability of GI products in post purchase.*

Because a significant proportion of respondents are dissatisfied with the ease of access to Geographical Indication Products, producers and marketers should consider expanding their marketing through various modes and channels, including digital and ecommerce platforms.

4.8.3 SATISFACTION LEVEL OF RESPONDENTS TOWARDS AFTER SALE SERVICES OF GI PRODUCTS

H7: CUSTOMERS ARE SATISFIED WITH AFTER SALES SERVICES OF GI PRODUCTS IN POST PURCHASE.

TABLE 4.26

FREQUENCY DISTRIBUTION OF RESPONDENTS' SATISFACTION TOWARDS 'AFTER SALE SERVICES OF GI PRODUCTS'

Level of Agreement	No. of respondents	Percent
Highly Satisfied (1)	44	7.8
Satisfied (2)	128	22.7
Neutral (3)	197	34.9
Dissatisfied (4)	156	27.6
Highly Dissatisfied (5)	40	7.1
Total	565	100.0

116

After sale Services

TABLE 4.27

ONE SAMPLE WILCOXON SIGNED RANK TEST RESULT

Wilcoxon signed- rank test			
Sign	**Obs**	**Sum ranks**	**Expected**
Positive	196	73902	70196
Negative	172	66490	70196
Zero	197	19503	19503
All	565	159895	159895

Unadjusted variance 15070104

Adjustment for ties   -489555

Adjustment for zeros -641973.75

Adjusted variance   13938575

Ho: varl = 3

      z   = 0.993

    prob > | z |= 0.3209

From the above one sample Wilcoxon signed rank test result (Table 4.28), it is observed that the p-value (0.3209) is greater than the significant at 5 percent level. Hence, the null hypothesis (H_0) that a higher proportion of respondents are remaining neutral to the above statement is accepted and alternative (H_1) is rejected. It observed from the above table that there are almost a similar number of respondents with a negative sign (172 respondents) and number of respondents with a positive sign [196 respondents].

Now, as the number of respondents with a negative sign (i.e, 172, 30.5 %) is closer to that of positive sign rank (196, 34.7%), one would conclude a same proportion of respondents under the sample study believes that *Customers are satisfied as well not satisfied with **After Sales services of GI** products in post purchase.* it is observed from the descriptive statistics (Table 30) that ***a considerable proportion*** of the respondents

117

Test Results

(34.9 percent) have remained neutral to the above statement thus not able to arrive at a definite conclusion that *they are satisfied as well not satisfied with **After Sales Service** of GI products in post purchase.*

Some Geographical Indication products have after-sale services that leave customers dissatisfied; therefore, it is the responsibility of producers to ensure that these products have adequate after-sale support; only then would it be feasible to retain existing customers.

4.8.4 TESTING RELATIONSHIP BETWEEN LEVEL OF CUSTOMER SATISFACTION AND AWARENESS OF RESPONDENTS

H₈: THERE IS A RELATION BETWEEN SATISFACTION LEVEL AND AWARENESS OF RESPONDENTS TOWARDS GI PRODUCTS.

TABLE 4.28

Correlations			
		Satisfaction level	Awareness
Satisfaction level	Pearson correlation	1	.838**
	Sig. (2-tailed)		.000
	N	565	565
Awareness	Pearson correlation	.838**	1
	Sig. (2-tailed)	.000	
	N	565	565
**. Correlation is significant at the 0.01 level (2-tailed).			

The provided correlation analysis assesses the relationship between the level of satisfaction and the awareness of customers regarding Geographical Indication (GI) products. The results indicate a strong positive correlation between these two variables. Specifically, the Pearson Correlation coefficient between satisfaction level and awareness is 0.838, which is highly significant at the 0.01 level (two-tailed). This suggests a robust

118

Awareness

and positive association between the level of satisfaction that customers experience with GI products and their awareness of these products. In other words, as customers become more aware of GI products, their satisfaction levels tend to increase. These findings imply that increasing customer awareness about GI products can have a positive impact on customer satisfaction. Businesses and organizations dealing with GI products may benefit from implementing strategies to enhance customer awareness, as it could lead to improved customer satisfaction and potentially greater loyalty to these products.

4.9 IMPACT OF GEOGRAPHICAL INDICATION LABELING ON CONSUMER BUYING BEHAVIOR

H₉: THERE IS AN IMPACT OF GEOGRAPHICAL INDICATION LABELING ON CONSUMER BUYING BEHAVIOR.

TABLE 4.29a

Model Summary				
Model	**R**	**R Square**	**Adjusted R Square**	**Std. Error of the Estimate**
1	.945[a]	.892	.892	.43981
a. Predictors: (Constant), customer buying behaviour				

TABLE 4.29b

Anova[a]						
	Model	**Sum of Squares**	**Df**	**Mean Square**	**F**	**Sig.**
1	Regression	904.052	2	904.052	4673.663	.000[b]
	Residual	108.904	563	.193		
	Total	1012.956	565			
A. Dependent Variable: geographical indicating labelling						
B. Predictors: (Constant), customer buying behaviour						

119

Impact

TABLE 4.29c

Coefficients[a]					
Model	Unstandardized Coefficients		Standardized Coefficients	T	Sig.
	B	Std. Error	Beta		
1 (Constant)	.222	.058		3.795	.000
1 Customer buying behaviour	.945	.014	.945	68.364	.000
A. Dependent Variable: geographical indicatoring labelling					

The conducted analysis delves into the influence of geographical indication (GI) labeling on consumer buying behavior. The results of the regression analysis reveal a robust and highly significant relationship between these two variables. The model's strong fit, indicated by an R-squared value of 0.892, suggests that approximately 89.2% of the variability in geographical indication labeling can be attributed to customer buying behavior as represented in the model. The ANOVA results further underscore the significance of this relationship, with a highly substantial F-statistic of 4673.663. The coefficients in the model confirm that customer buying behavior plays a pivotal role, with a Beta coefficient of 0.945, signifying a strong positive association. This implies that as customer buying behavior increases, there is a pronounced tendency for consumers to respond positively to products bearing geographical indication labels. These findings underscore the importance for businesses and organizations involved in marketing such labeled products to understand and influence customer buying behavior, as it holds a substantial sway over consumer preferences and responses to GI-labeled items.

121

Anova

4.10 TESTING OF REALATIONSHIP BETWEEN PROBLEMS RELATING TO PURCHASE OF GI PRODUCTS AND LEVEL OF CUSTOMER SATISFACTION

H_{10} : **PROBLEMS RELATING TO GI PRODUCTS PURCHASE HAVING AN IMPACT ON CUSTOMER SATISFACTION**

TABLE 4.30

Correlations		Satisfaction level	Problem faced
Satisfaction level	Pearson Correlation	1	.544[**]
	Sig. (2-tailed)		.000
	N	565	565
Problem faced	Pearson Correlation	.544[**]	1
	Sig. (2-tailed)	.000	
	N	565	565
[**]. Correlation is significant at the 0.01 level (2-tailed).			

The correlation analysis conducted examines the relationship between the level of satisfaction and the problems faced by customers related to Geographical Indication (GI) products. The results indicate a significant positive correlation between these two variables. Specifically, the Pearson Correlation coefficient between satisfaction level and problems faced is 0.544, which is highly significant at the 0.01 level (two-tailed). This suggests a meaningful and positive association between the level of satisfaction that customers experience with GI products and the problems they encounter when dealing with these products. In simpler terms, as customers face fewer problems related to GI products, their satisfaction levels tend to increase. These findings imply that addressing and resolving issues or challenges that customers encounter when dealing with GI products can have a positive impact on customer satisfaction. Businesses and organizations involved in the production and distribution of GI products should consider strategies to minimize customer problems and enhance their overall satisfaction. This could lead to improved customer loyalty and positive word-of-mouth recommendations.

121

Impact on customer satisfaction

4.11 INFERENTIAL STATISTICS RESULTS

An attempt is made to compare on whether there are any changes in level of agreement with regard to dimensions namely *Economic Factor, Socio-cultural Factor, Psychological Factor* **and** *Personal factor* on various socio-demographical variables of the respondents.

4.11.1 GENDER

4.12.1.1 TESTING OF DIFFERENCE BETWEEN FACTORS INFLUENCING THE PURCHASE OF GI PRODUCTS AND GENDER OF THE RESPONDENTS

H_{11}: THERE IS A SIGNIFICANT DIFFERENCE IN THE MEAN SCORE BETWEEN ECONOMIC FACTOR AND GENDER OF THE RESPONDENTS

TABLE 4.31

INDEPENDENT T-TEST

Dimension	Gender	N	Mean	SD	t-value	p-value
Economic Factor	Male	282	2.172	0.849	0.457	0.648
	Female	283	2.139	0.836		

Firstly, it is observed from the independent t-test result depicted in Table 4.32 that there is no significant difference in mean rating scores of level of agreement between Male and Female educators with respect to dimension Economic Factor (t= 0.457, p=0.648, p>0.05) at 5% level of significance. Hence, the null hypothesis is accepted and alternative hypothesis is rejected. In essence, there is no statistical evidence to conclude that there is a significant difference in the mean scores rated by both male and female customers with respect to economic factor.

122

Economivc factors

75

H$_{12}$: THERE IS A SIGNIFICANT DIFFERENCE IN THE MEAN SCORE BETWEEN SOCIO-CULTURAL FACTOR AND GENDER OF THE RESPONDENTS

TABLE 4.32

INDEPENDENT T-TEST

Dimension	Gender	N	Mean	SD	t-value	p-value
Socio-Cultural factor	Male	282	2.140	0.855	0.548	0.433
	Female	283	2.084	0.838		

It is observed from the independent t-test result depicted in Table 4.33 that there is no significant difference in mean rating scores of level of agreement between Male and Female educators with respect to dimension namely Socio-Cultural factor (t= 0.548, p=0.433, p>0.05), at 5% level of significance. Hence, the null hypothesis is accepted and alternative hypothesis is rejected. In essence, there is no statistical evidence to conclude that there is a significant difference in the mean scores rated by both male and female customers with respect to Socio-cultural factor.

123

Socio cultural factors

H$_{13}$: THERE IS A SIGNIFICANT DIFFERENCE IN THE MEAN SCORE BETWEEN

PSYCHOLOGICAL FACTOR AND GENDER OF THE RESPONDENTS

TABLE 4.33

INDEPENDENT T-TEST

Dimension	Gender	N	Mean	SD	t-value	p-value
Psychological Factor	Male	282	2.098	0.880	0.750	0.912
	Female	283	2.090	0.869		

It is observed from the independent t-test result depicted in Table 4.34 that there is no significant difference in mean rating scores of level of agreement between Male and Female educators with respect to dimension Psychological factor (t= 0.750, p=0.912, p>0.05), at 5% level of significance. Hence, the null hypothesis is accepted and alternative hypothesis is rejected. In essence, there is no statistical evidence to conclude that there is a significant difference in the mean scores rated by both male and female customers with respect to Psychological factor.

124

Psychological factors

H$_{14}$: THERE IS A SIGNIFICANT DIFFERENCE IN THE MEAN SCORE BETWEEN

PERSONAL FACTOR AND GENDER OF THE RESPONDENTS

TABLE 4.34

INDEPENDENT T-TEST

Dimension	Gender	N	Mean	SD	t-value	p-value
Personal factor	Male	282	2.138	1.017	0.571	0.932
	Female	283	2.129	0.962		

It is observed from the independent t-test result depicted in Table 4.35 that there is no significant difference in mean rating scores of level of agreement between Male and Female educators with respect to dimension Personal factor (t= 0.571, p=0.932, p>0.05), at 5% level of significance. Hence, the null hypothesis is accepted and alternative hypothesis is rejected. In essence, there is no statistical evidence to conclude that there is a significant difference in the mean scores rated by both male and female customers with respect to Personal factor.

125

Personal factor

H$_{15}$: THERE IS A SIGNIFICANT DIFFERENCE IN THE MEAN SCORE BETWEEN

PURCHASE INTENTION AND GENDER OF THE RESPONDENTS

TABLE 4.35

INDEPENDENT T-TEST

Dimension	Gender	N	Mean	SD	t-value	p-value
Purchase intention	Male	282	2.486	0.990	0.232	0.911
	Female	283	2.479	0.966		

It is observed from the independent t-test result depicted in Table 4.36 that there is no significant difference in mean rating scores of level of agreement between Male and Female educators with respect to dimension Purchase intention (t= 0.232, p=0.911, p>0.05) at 5% level of significance. Hence, the null hypothesis is accepted and alternative hypothesis is rejected. In essence, there is no statistical evidence to conclude that there is a significant difference in the mean scores rated by both male and female customers with respect to Purchase intention.

126

Purchase intention

4.11.2.1 TESTING OF DIFFERENCE BETWEEN FACTORS INFLUENCING THE PURCHASE OF GI PRODUCTS AND AGE OF THE RESPONDENTS

H_{16}: THERE IS A SIGNIFICANT DIFFERENCE IN THE MEAN SCORE BETWEEN ECONOMIC FACTOR AND AGE OF THE RESPONDENTS

TABLE 4.36

ONE-WAY ANOVA BETWEEN ECONOMIC FACTOR AND AGE

	Sum of Squares	Df	Mean Square	F	p-value
Between Groups	2.367	3	0.789	1.113	0.343
Within Groups	397.629	561	0.709		
Total	399.996	564			

It is observed from the one way ANOVA result depicted in Table 4.37 that the p-value of Economic factor (0.343) is greater than the significance alpha level of 0.05. Thus, it is concluded that there is no significant (statistically) difference in mean rating scores of level of agreement across four categories of age group (21 to 30 years, 31 to 40 years, 41 to 50 years and greater than 50 years) of customers with respect to above dimensions at 5% level of significance. Hence, the null hypothesis is accepted and alternative hypothesis is rejected. In a sense, the mean score of the Economic Factor, do not significantly differ between the customers with less than 30 years of age group and customers with 31 to 40 years of age group, between the customers with 41 to 50 years and more than 50 years of age group

127

Factors Influencing

H[17]: THERE IS A SIGNIFICANT DIFFERENCE IN THE MEAN SCORE BETWEEN

SOCIO-CULTURAL FACTOR AND AGE OF THE RESPONDENTS.

TABLE 4.37

ONE-WAY ANOVA BETWEEN SOCIO-CULTURAL FACTOR AND AGE

	Sum of Squares	Df	Mean Square	F	p-value
Between Groups	1.732	3	0.577	0.806	0.491
Within Groups	401.966	561	0.717		
Total	403.697	564			

It is observed from the one way ANOVA result depicted in Table 4.38 that the p-value of Socio-Cultural factor (0.491) is greater than the significance alpha level of 0.05. Thus, it is concluded that there is no significant (statistically) difference in mean rating scores of level of agreement across four categories of age group (21 to 30 years, 31 to 40 years, 41 to 50 years and greater than 50 years) of customers with respect to above dimensions at 5% level of significance. Hence, the null hypothesis is accepted and alternative hypothesis is rejected. In a sense, the mean score of the Socio-Cultural Factor, do not significantly differ between the customers with less than 30 years of age group and customers with 31 to 40 years of age group, between the customers with 41 to 50 years and more than 50 years of age group.

128

Socio Cultural

H[18]: THERE IS A SIGNIFICANT DIFFERENCE IN THE MEAN SCORE BETWEEN

PSYCHOLOGICAL FACTOR AND AGE OF THE RESPONDENTS

TABLE 4.38

ONE-WAY ANOVA BETWEEN PSYCHOLOGICAL FACTOR AND AGE

	Sum of Squares	Df	Mean Square	F	p-value
Between Groups	1.155	3	0.385	0.503	0.681
Within Groups	429.594	561	0.766		
Total	430.748	564			

It is observed from the one way ANOVA result depicted in Table 4.39 that the p-value of Psychological factor (0.681) is greater than the significance alpha level of 0.05. Thus, it is concluded that there is no significant (statistically) difference in mean rating scores of level of agreement across four categories of age group (21 to 30 years, 31 to 40 years, 41 to 50 years and greater than 50 years) of customers with respect to above dimensions at 5% level of significance. Hence, the null hypothesis is accepted and alternative hypothesis is rejected. In a sense, the mean score of the Psychological Factor, do not significantly differ between the customers with less than 30 years of age group and customers with 31 to 40 years of age group, between the customers with 41 to 50 years and more than 50 years of age group.

129

Psychological

H$_{19}$: THERE IS A SIGNIFICANT DIFFERENCE IN THE MEAN SCORE BETWEEN **PERSONAL FACTOR AND AGE OF THE RESPONDENTS.**

TABLE 4.39

ONE-WAY ANOVA BETWEEN AGE GROUP AND PERSONAL FACTOR

	Sum of Squares	Df	Mean Square	F	p-value
Between Groups	2.379	3	0.793	0.830	0.478
Within Groups	536.194	561	0.956		
Total	538.573	564			

It is observed from the one way ANOVA result depicted in Table 4.40 that the p-value of Personal factor (0.478) is greater than the significance alpha level of 0.05. Thus, it is concluded that there is no significant (statistically) difference in mean rating scores of level of agreement across four categories of age group (21 to 30 years, 31 to 40 years, 41 to 50 years and greater than 50 years) of customers with respect to above dimensions at 5% level of significance. Hence, the null hypothesis is accepted and alternative hypothesis is rejected. In a sense, the mean score of the Personal Factor, do not significantly differ between the customers with less than 30 years of age group and customers with 31 to 40 years of age group, between the customers with 41 to 50 years and more than 50 years of age group.

131

Age Group

H$_{20}$: THERE IS A SIGNIFICANT DIFFERENCE IN THE MEAN SCORE BETWEEN

PURCHASE INTENTION AND AGE OF THE RESPONDENTS

TABLE 4.40 ONE-WAY ANOVA BETWEEN AGE GROUP AND PURCHASE INTENTION					
	Sum of Squares	**Df**	**Mean Square**	**F**	**p-value**
Between Groups	3.199	3	1.066	1.091	0.352
Within Groups	548.337	561	0.977		
Total	551.536	564			

It is observed from the one way ANOVA result depicted in Table 4.41 that the p-value of Purchase Intention 0.352) is greater than the significance alpha level of 0.05. Thus, it is concluded that there is no significant (statistically) difference in mean rating scores of level of agreement across four categories of age group (21 to 30 years, 31 to 40 years, 41 to 50 years and greater than 50 years) of customers with respect to above dimensions at 5% level of significance. Hence, the null hypothesis is accepted and alternative hypothesis is rejected. In a sense, the mean score of the Purchase Intention, do not significantly differ between the customers with less than 30 years of age group and customers with 31 to 40 years of age group, between the customers with 41 to 50 years and more than 50 years of age group.

131

Purchase Intention

4.11.2.3 TESTING OF DIFFERENCE BETWEEN AGE OF THE RESPONDENTS AND THEIR LEVEL OF SATISFACTION TOWARDS GI PRODUCTS

H$_{21}$: THERE IS A SIGNIFICANT DIFFERENCE BETWEEN AGE OF THE RESPONDENTS AND THEIR LEVEL OF SATISFACTION TOWRADS GI PRODUCTS.

TABLE 4.41(a)

ANOVA					
Satisfaction level					
	Sum of Squares	df	Mean Square	F	Sig.
Between Groups	984.956	4	328.319	6578.097	.000
Within Groups	28.000	561	.050		
Total	1012.956	565			

TABLE 4.41(b)

Multiple Comparisons							
Dependent Variable: satisfaction level							
	(I) age of the respondent	(J) age of the respondent	Mean Difference (I-J)	Std. Error	Sig.	95% Confidence Interval	
						Lower Bound	Upper Bound
Tukey HSD	less than 30	30-40	.00000	.03656	1.000	-.0942	.0942
		50 and above	-2.50000*	.02985	.000	-2.5769	-2.4231
		5.00	-3.00000*	.02492	.000	-3.0642	-2.9358
	30-40	less than 30	.00000	.03656	1.000	-.0942	.0942
		50 and above	-2.50000*	.03656	.000	-2.5942	-2.4058
		5.00	-3.00000*	.03266	.000	-3.0841	-2.9159

132

Level of satisfaction

			Mean Diff	Std. Error	Sig.	Lower	Upper
	50 and above	less than 30	2.50000*	.02985	.000	2.4231	2.5769
		30-40	2.50000*	.03656	.000	2.4058	2.5942
		5.00	-.50000*	.02492	.000	-.5642	-.4358
	5.00	less than 30	3.00000*	.02492	.000	2.9358	3.0642
		30-40	3.00000*	.03266	.000	2.9159	3.0841
		50 and above	.50000*	.02492	.000	.4358	.5642
LSD	less than 30	30-40	.00000	.03656	1.000	-.0718	.0718
		50 and above	-2.50000*	.02985	.000	-2.5586	-2.4414
		5.00	-3.00000*	.02492	.000	-3.0489	-2.9511
	30-40	less than 30	.00000	.03656	1.000	-.0718	.0718
		50 and above	-2.50000*	.03656	.000	-2.5718	-2.4282
		5.00	-3.00000*	.03266	.000	-3.0641	-2.9359
	50 and above	less than 30	2.50000*	.02985	.000	2.4414	2.5586
		30-40	2.50000*	.03656	.000	2.4282	2.5718
		5.00	-.50000*	.02492	.000	-.5489	-.4511
	5.00	less than 30	3.00000*	.02492	.000	2.9511	3.0489
		30-40	3.00000*	.03266	.000	2.9359	3.0641
		50 and above	.50000*	.02492	.000	.4511	.5489
TAMHANE	less than 30	30-40	.00000	.00000	.	.0000	.0000
		50 and above	-2.50000*	.04746	.000	-2.6271	-2.3729
		5.00	-3.00000	.00000	.	-3.0000	-3.0000
	30-40	less than 30	.00000	.00000	.	.0000	.0000
		50 and above	-2.50000*	.04746	.000	-2.6271	-2.3729
		5.00	-3.00000	.00000	.	-3.0000	-3.0000
	50 and above	less than 30	2.50000*	.04746	.000	2.3729	2.6271

133

Tavble

85

		30-40	2.50000[*]	.04746	.000	2.3729	2.6271
		5.00	-.50000[*]	.04746	.000	-.6271	-.3729
		less than 30	3.00000	.00000	.	3.0000	3.0000
	5.00	30-40	3.00000	.00000	.	3.0000	3.0000
		50 and above	.50000[*]	.04746	.000	.3729	.6271
*. The mean difference is significant at the 0.05 level.							

The analysis investigates the relationship between satisfaction levels towards geographical indication products and the age of respondents using an ANOVA. The results reveal an extremely significant overall difference in satisfaction levels based on age groups, with a very low p-value of less than 0.001. This suggests that age significantly influences how individuals perceive and rate their satisfaction with geographical indication products. Further examination through multiple comparisons, employing various methods including Tukey HSD, LSD, and Tamhane, provides detailed insights into specific differences between age groups. Notably, older respondents (aged 50 and above) consistently report significantly lower satisfaction levels than their younger counterparts (less than 30 and 30-40), with substantial mean differences. Additionally, respondents aged 5 years also exhibit lower satisfaction levels than younger age groups. These findings suggest that there is a pronounced association between age and satisfaction levels regarding geographical indication products, with older individuals expressing lower levels of satisfaction. This information can be valuable for businesses and producers of geographical indication products when targeting and catering to different age segments in their marketing and product development efforts. It implies the need for customized strategies to enhance satisfaction levels, particularly among older consumers.

134

Results

4.11.3.1 TESTING OF DIFFERENCE BETWEEN MONTHLY INCOME OF THE RESPONDENTS AND FACTORS INFUENCING THE PURCHASE OF THE GI PRODUCTS

H_{22}: THERE IS A SIGNIFICANT DIFFERENCE IN THE MEAN SCORE BETWEEN ECONOMIC FACTOR AND MONTHLY INCOME OF THE RESPONDENTS

TABLE 4.42						
ONE-WAY ANOVA BETWEEN MONTHLY INCOME AND ECONOMIC FACTOR						
Particulars	**Sum of Squares**	**Df**	**Mean Square**	**F**	**p-value**
Between Groups	0.861	3	0.287	0.403	0.751
Within Groups	399.135	561	0.711		
Total	399.996	564			

It is observed from the one way ANOVA result depicted in Table 4.43 that the p-value of Economic Factor (0.751) is greater than the significance alpha level of 0.05. Thus, it is concluded that there is no significant (statistically) difference in mean rating scores of level of agreement across *four levels* of Monthly Income of customers with respect to above dimensions at 5% level of significance. Hence, the null hypothesis is accepted and alternative hypothesis is rejected. In a sense, the mean score of the *Economic Factor* do not significantly differ between the customers with *less than* Rs 10,000 *and customers with Rs 10,000-20,000 of Monthly Income, between the customers with* 20,000- 30,000 *of Monthly Income and more than Rs* 30,000 of monthly *Income of customers.* The perception pertaining to Economic Factor remains the same irrespective the category of monthly income of the customers.

135

Economic factors

H$_{23}$: THERE IS A SIGNIFICANT DIFFERENCE IN THE MEAN SCORE BETWEEN SOCIO-CULTURAL FACTOR AND MONTHLY INCOME OF THE RESPONDENTS

| **TABLE 4.43** ||||||
| **ONE-WAY ANOVA BETWEEN MONTHLY INCOME AND SOCIO-CULTURAL FACTOR** ||||||
Particulars	**Sum of Squares**	**Df**	**Mean Square**	**F**	**p-value**
Between Groups	0.336	3	0.112	0.156	0.926
Within Groups	403.361	561	0.719		
Total	403.697	564			

It is observed from the one way ANOVA result depicted in Table 4.44 that the p-value of Socio-Cultural Factor (0.926) is greater than the significance alpha level of 0.05. Thus, it is concluded that there is no significant (statistically) difference in mean rating scores of level of agreement across *four levels* of Monthly Income of customers with respect to above dimensions at 5% level of significance. Hence, the null hypothesis is accepted and alternative hypothesis is rejected. In a sense, the mean score of the Socio-Cultural Factor do not significantly differ between the customers with *less than* Rs 10,000 *and customers with Rs* 10,000-20,000 *of Monthly Income, between the customers with* 20,000-30,000 *of Monthly Income and more than Rs* 30,000 of monthly *Income of customers*. The perception pertaining to Socio-Cultural Factor remains the same irrespective the category of monthly income of the customers.

136

Socio Cultural factors

H_{24} THERE IS A SIGNIFICANT DIFFERENCE IN THE MEAN SCORE BETWEEN PSYCHOLOGICAL FACTOR AND MONTHLY INCOME OF THE RESPONDENTS.

TABLE 4.44

ONE-WAY ANOVA BETWEEN MONTHLY INCOME AND PSYCHOLOGICAL FACTOR

Particulars	Sum of Squares	Df	Mean Square	F	p-value
Between Groups	0.927	3	0.309	0.403	0.751
Within Groups	429.821	561	0.766		
Total	430.748	564			

It is observed from the one way ANOVA result depicted in Table 4.45 that the p-value of Psychological Factor (0.751) is greater than the significance alpha level of 0.05. Thus, it is concluded that there is no significant (statistically) difference in mean rating scores of level of agreement across *four levels* of Monthly Income of customers with respect to above dimensions at 5% level of significance. Hence, the null hypothesis is accepted and alternative hypothesis is rejected. In a sense, the mean score of the Psychological Factor do not significantly differ between the customers with *less than* Rs 10,000 *and customers with Rs* 10,000-20,000 *of Monthly Income, between the customers with* 20,000-30,000 *of Monthly Income and more than Rs* 30,000 of monthly *Income of customers*. The perception pertaining to Psychological Factor remains the same irrespective the category of monthly income of the customers.

137

Psychological factor

H$_{25}$: THERE IS A SIGNIFICANT DIFFERENCE IN THE MEAN SCORE BETWEEN PERSONAL FACTOR AND MONTHLY INCOME OF THE RESPONDENTS.

TABLE 4.45					
ONE-WAY ANOVA BETWEEN MONTHLY INCOME AND PERSONAL FACTOR					
Particulars	**Sum of Squares**	**Df**	**Mean Square**	**F**	**p-value**
Between Groups	3.558	3	1.186	1.244	0.293
Within Groups	535.015	561	0.954		
Total	538.573	564			

It is observed from the one way ANOVA result depicted in Table 4.46 that the p-value of Personal Factor (0.293) is greater than the significance alpha level of 0.05. Thus, it is concluded that there is no significant (statistically) difference in mean rating scores of level of agreement across *four levels* of Monthly Income of customers with respect to above dimensions at 5% level of significance. Hence, the null hypothesis is accepted and alternative hypothesis is rejected. In a sense, the mean score of the Personal Factor do not significantly differ between the customers with *less than* Rs 10,000 *and customers with Rs* 10,000-20,000 *of Monthly Income, between the customers with* 20,000- 30,000 *of Monthly Income and more than Rs* 30,000 of monthly *Income of customers.* The perception pertaining to Personal Factor remains the same irrespective the category of monthly income of the customers.

138

Personal factor

H$_{26}$: THERE IS A SIGNIFICANT DIFFERENCE IN THE MEAN SCORE BETWEEN PURCHASE INTENTION AND MONTHLY INCOME OF THE RESPONDENTS.

TABLE 4.46					
ONE-WAY ANOVA BETWEEN MONTHLY INCOME AND PURCHASE INTENTION					
Particulars	**Sum of Squares**	**Df**	**Mean Square**	**F**	**p-value**
Between Groups	0.83	3	0.277	0.282	0.838
Within Groups	550.706	561	0.982		
Total	551.536	564			

It is observed from the one way ANOVA result depicted in Table 4.47 that the p-value of Purchase Intention (0.838) is greater than the significance alpha level of 0.05. Thus, it is concluded that there is no significant (statistically) difference in mean rating scores of level of agreement across *four levels* of Monthly Income of customers with respect to above dimensions at 5% level of significance. Hence, the null hypothesis is accepted and alternative hypothesis is rejected. In a sense, the mean score of the Purchase Intention do not significantly differ between the customers with *less than* Rs 10,000 *and customers with Rs* 10,000-20,000 *of Monthly Income, between the customers with* 20,000-30,000 *of Monthly Income and more than Rs* 30,000 of monthly *Income of customers.* The perception pertaining to Purchase Intention remains the same irrespective the category of monthly income of the customers.

139

Purchase intention

4.11.4 EDUCATIONAL STATUS

4.11.4.1 TESTING OF THE DIFFERENCE BETWEEN EDUCATIONAL STATUS AND FACTORS INFLUENCING THE PURCHASE OF GI PRODUCTS

H_{27}: THERE IS A SIGNIFICANT DIFFERENCE IN THE MEAN SCORE BETWEEN ECONOMIC FACTOR AND EDUCATIONAL STATUS OF THE RESPONDENTS.

TABLE 4.47

ONE-WAY ANOVA BETWEEN EDUCATIONAL STATUS AND ECONOMIC FACTOR

Particulars	Sum of Squares	Df	Mean Square	F	p-value
Between Groups	2.039	4	0.51	0.717	0.580
Within Groups	397.957	560	0.711		
Total	399.996	564			

It is observed from the one way ANOVA result depicted in Table 4.48 that the p-value of Economic Factor (0.580) greater than the significance alpha level of 0.05. Thus, it is concluded that there is no significant (statistically) difference in mean rating scores of level of agreement across *four levels of* educational status of customers with respect to above dimensions at 5% level of significance. Hence, the null hypothesis is accepted and alternative hypothesis is rejected. In a sense, the mean score of the *Economic Factor* do not significantly differ between the customers with *graduation, between the customers with graduation and customers having post-graduation qualification.* The perception pertaining to Economic Factor remains the same irrespective of the educational status of the customers.

141

Economic factor

H$_{28}$: THERE IS A SIGNIFICANT DIFFERENCE IN THE MEAN SCORE BETWEEN SOCIO-CULTURAL FACTOR AND EDUCATIONAL STATUS OF THE RESPONDENTS.

<table>
<tr><td colspan="6">TABLE 4.48
ONE-WAY ANOVA BETWEEN EDUCATIONAL STATUS AND SOCIO-CULTURAL FACTOR</td></tr>
<tr><td>Particulars</td><td>Sum of Squares</td><td>Df</td><td>Mean Square</td><td>F</td><td>p-value</td></tr>
<tr><td>Between Groups</td><td>1.467</td><td>4</td><td>0.367</td><td>0.511</td><td>0.728</td></tr>
<tr><td>Within Groups</td><td>402.23</td><td>560</td><td>0.718</td><td></td><td></td></tr>
<tr><td>Total</td><td>403.697</td><td>564</td><td></td><td></td><td></td></tr>
</table>

It is observed from the one way ANOVA result depicted in Table 4.49 that the p-value of Socio Cultural Factor (0.728) greater than the significance alpha level of 0.05. Thus, it is concluded that there is no significant (statistically) difference in mean rating scores of level of agreement across *four levels of* educational status of customers with respect to above dimensions at 5% level of significance. Hence, the null hypothesis is accepted and alternative hypothesis is rejected. In a sense, the mean score of the Socio Cultural *Factor* do not significantly differ between the customers with *graduation, between the customers with graduation and customers having post-graduation qualification.* The perception pertaining to Socio Cultural Factor remains the same irrespective of the educational status of the customers.

141

Socio cultural factors

94

H$_{39}$: THERE IS A SIGNIFICANT DIFFERENCE IN THE MEAN SCORE BETWEEN PSYCHOLOGICAL FACTOR AND EDUCATIONAL STATUS OF THE RESPONDENTS.

TABLE 4.49

ONE-WAY ANOVA BETWEEN EDUCATIONAL STATUS AND PSYCHOLOGICAL FACTOR

Particulars	Sum of Squares	Df	Mean Square	F	p-value
Between Groups	5.338	4	1.335	1.757	0.136
Within Groups	425.41	560	0.76		
Total	430.748	564			

It is observed from the one way ANOVA result depicted in Table 4.51 that the p-value of Psychological Factor (0.136) greater than the significance alpha level of 0.05. Thus, it is concluded that there is no significant (statistically) difference in mean rating scores of level of agreement across *four levels of* educational status of customers with respect to above dimensions at 5% level of significance. Hence, the null hypothesis is accepted and alternative hypothesis is rejected. In a sense, the mean score of the Psychological *Factor* do not significantly differ between the customers with *graduation, between the customers with graduation and customers having post-graduation qualification.* The perception pertaining to Psychological Factor remains the same irrespective of the educational status of the customers.

142

Educational status

H$_{30}$: THERE IS A SIGNIFICANT DIFFERENCE IN THE MEAN SCORE BETWEEN PERSONAL FACTOR AND EDUCATIONAL STATUS OF THE RESPONDENTS.

TABLE 4.50

ONE-WAY ANOVA BETWEEN EDUCATIONAL STATUS AND PERSONAL FACTOR

Particulars	Sum of Squares	Df	Mean Square	F	p-value
Between Groups	6.37	4	1.593	1.688	0.151
Within Groups	528.203	560	0.943		
Total	534.573	564			

It is observed from the one way ANOVA result depicted in Table 4.51 that the p-value of Personal Factor (0.151) greater than the significance alpha level of 0.05. Thus, it is concluded that there is no significant (statistically) difference in mean rating scores of level of agreement across *four levels of* educational status of customers with respect to above dimensions at 5% level of significance. Hence, the null hypothesis is accepted and alternative hypothesis is rejected. In a sense, the mean score of the Personal *Factor* do not significantly differ between the customers with *graduation, between the customers with graduation and customers having post-graduation qualification.* The perception pertaining to Personal Factor remains the same irrespective of the educational status of the customers.

143

Personal factor

H_{31}: THERE IS A SIGNIFICANT DIFFERENCE IN THE MEAN SCORE BETWEEN PURCHASE INTENTION AND EDUCATIONAL STATUS OF THE RESPONDENTS.

TABLE 4.51

ONE-WAY ANOVA BETWEEN EDUCATIONAL STATUS AND PURCHASE INTENTION

Particulars	Sum of Squares	Df	Mean Square	F	p-value
Between Groups	4.001	4	1	1.023	0.395
Within Groups	547.535	560	0.978		
Total	551.536	564			

It is observed from the one way ANOVA result depicted in Table 4.52 that the p-value of Purchase Intention (0.395) greater than the significance alpha level of 0.05. Thus, it is concluded that there is no significant (statistically) difference in mean rating scores of level of agreement across *four levels of* educational status of customers with respect to above dimensions at 5% level of significance. Hence, the null hypothesis is accepted and alternative hypothesis is rejected. In a sense, the mean score of the Purchase Intention do not significantly differ between the customers with *graduation, between the customers with graduation and customers having post-graduation qualification.* The perception pertaining to Purchase Intention remains the same irrespective of the educational status of the customers.

144

Purchase intention

4.11.4.2 TESTING OF THE DIFFERENCE BETWEEN LEVEL OF CUSTOMER SATISFACTION AND EDUCATION LEVEL OF THE RESPONDENTS

H_{32}: THERE IS A SIGNIFICANT DIFFERENCE BETWEEN LEVEL OF CUSTOMER SATISFACTION AND EDUCATION LEVEL OF THE RESPONDENTS

TABLE 4.52 (a)

ANOVA					
Satisfaction level					
Particulars	Sum of squares	Df	Mean square	F	Sig.
Between groups	900.956	5	225.239	1126.195	.000
Within groups	112.000	560	.200		
Total	1012.956	565			

TABLE 4.52 (b)

Multiple comparisons							
Dependent variable: satisfaction level							
	(I) Educational qualification	(j) Educational qualification	Mean difference (i-j)	Std. Error	Sig.	95% confidence interval	
						Lower bound	Upper bound
TUKEY HSD	Illiterate	Primary	.00000	.08452	1.000	-.2313	.2313
		Highschool	-1.00000*	.07319	.000	-1.2003	-.7997
		Graduate	-3.00000*	.06891	.000	-3.1886	-2.8114
		Post graduate	-3.00000*	.06886	.000	-3.1884	-2.8116
	Primary	Illiterate	.00000	.08452	1.000	-.2313	.2313
		Highschool	-1.00000*	.07319	.000	-1.2003	-.7997
		Graduate	-3.00000*	.06891	.000	-3.1886	-2.8114
		Post graduate	-3.00000*	.06886	.000	-3.1884	-2.8116
	Highschool	Illiterate	1.00000*	.07319	.000	.7997	1.2003
		Primary	1.00000*	.07319	.000	.7997	1.2003
		Graduate	-2.00000*	.05443	.000	-2.1489	-1.8511
		Post graduate	-2.00000*	.05436	.000	-2.1488	-1.8512

145

Education level

Multiple comparisons							
Dependent variable: satisfaction level							
	(I) Educational qualification	(j) Educational qualification	Mean difference (i-j)	Std. Error	Sig.	95% confidence interval	
						Lower bound	Upper bound
LSD	Graduate	Illiterate	3.00000*	.06891	.000	2.8114	3.1886
		Primary	3.00000*	.06891	.000	2.8114	3.1886
		Highschool	2.00000*	.05443	.000	1.8511	2.1489
		Post graduate	.00000	.04844	1.000	-.1326	.1326
	Post graduate	Illiterate	3.00000*	.06886	.000	2.8116	3.1884
		Primary	3.00000*	.06886	.000	2.8116	3.1884
		Highschool	2.00000*	.05436	.000	1.8512	2.1488
		Graduate	.00000	.04844	1.000	-.1326	.1326
	Illiterate	Primary	.00000	.08452	1.000	-.1660	.1660
		Highschool	-1.00000*	.07319	.000	-1.1438	-.8562
		Graduate	-3.00000*	.06891	.000	-3.1353	-2.8647
		Post graduate	-3.00000*	.06886	.000	-3.1352	-2.8648
	Primary	Illiterate	.00000	.08452	1.000	-.1660	.1660
		Highschool	-1.00000*	.07319	.000	-1.1438	-.8562
		Graduate	-3.00000*	.06891	.000	-3.1353	-2.8647
		Post graduate	-3.00000*	.06886	.000	-3.1352	-2.8648
	Highschool	Illiterate	1.00000*	.07319	.000	.8562	1.1438
		Primary	1.00000*	.07319	.000	.8562	1.1438
		Graduate	-2.00000*	.05443	.000	-2.1069	-1.8931
		Post graduate	-2.00000*	.05436	.000	-2.1068	-1.8932
	Graduate	Illiterate	3.00000*	.06891	.000	2.8647	3.1353
		Primary	3.00000*	.06891	.000	2.8647	3.1353
		Highschool	2.00000*	.05443	.000	1.8931	2.1069
		Post graduate	.00000	.04844	1.000	-.0951	.0951
	Post graduate	Illiterate	3.00000*	.06886	.000	2.8648	3.1352
		Primary	3.00000*	.06886	.000	2.8648	3.1352
		Highschool	2.00000*	.05436	.000	1.8932	2.1068
		Graduate	.00000	.04844	1.000	-.0951	.0951
TAMHANE	Illiterate	Primary	.00000	.00000	.	.0000	.0000
		Highschool	-1.00000*	.09492	.000	-1.2711	-.7289

146

Table

Multiple comparisons							
Dependent variable: satisfaction level							
(I) Educational qualification	(j) Educational qualification	Mean difference (i-j)	Std. Error	Sig.	95% confidence interval	
					Lower bound	Upper bound
		Graduate	-3.00000	.00000	.	-3.0000	-3.0000
		Post graduate	-3.00000	.00000	.	-3.0000	-3.0000
Primary		Illiterate	.00000	.00000	.	.0000	.0000
		Highschool	-1.00000*	.09492	.000	-1.2711	-.7289
		Graduate	-3.00000	.00000	.	-3.0000	-3.0000
		Post graduate	-3.00000	.00000	.	-3.0000	-3.0000
Highschool		Illiterate	1.00000*	.09492	.000	.7289	1.2711
		Primary	1.00000*	.09492	.000	.7289	1.2711
		Graduate	-2.00000*	.09492	.000	-2.2711	-1.7289
		Post graduate	-2.00000*	.09492	.000	-2.2711	-1.7289
Graduate		Illiterate	3.00000	.00000	.	3.0000	3.0000
		Primary	3.00000	.00000	.	3.0000	3.0000
		Highschool	2.00000*	.09492	.000	1.7289	2.2711
		Post graduate	.00000	.00000	.	.0000	.0000
Post graduate		Illiterate	3.00000	.00000	.	3.0000	3.0000
		Primary	3.00000	.00000	.	3.0000	3.0000
		Highschool	2.00000*	.09492	.000	1.7289	2.2711
		Graduate	.00000	.00000	.	.0000	.0000

*. The mean difference is significant at the 0.05 level.

The analysis conducted explores the relationship between the educational qualifications of customers and their satisfaction levels concerning Geographical Indication (GI) products. The results of the analysis, which employs an Analysis of Variance (ANOVA) test, reveal a significant relationship between these two variables. The ANOVA results indicate that there is a substantial variation in satisfaction levels among customers with different educational qualifications. The between-groups variance is statistically significant, with an F-statistic of 1126.195 and a corresponding p-value of less than 0.001. This suggests that educational qualifications have a considerable impact on customers'

147

Results

satisfaction levels when it comes to GI products. To further understand the specific differences in satisfaction levels among different educational groups, multiple comparison tests were conducted using methods such as Tukey's Honestly Significant Difference (HSD), LSD (Least Significant Difference), and Tamhane's T2. These tests confirmed significant mean differences in satisfaction levels between various educational groups. The findings indicate that customers with different educational qualifications tend to have varying levels of satisfaction with GI products. This implies that businesses and organizations involved in the production and marketing of GI products should consider tailoring their strategies and communication to meet the specific needs and preferences of customers from different educational backgrounds to enhance overall customer satisfaction and loyalty.

4.12 LOCALITY

4.12.1 TESTING OF DIFFERENCE BETWEEN TYPE OF LOCALITY AND BUYING FREQUENCY

H_{33}: THERE IS A SIGNIFICANT DIFFERENCE BETWEEN TYPE OF LOCALITY AND BUYING FREQUENCY OF THE RESPONDETS.

TYPE OF LOCALITY AND BUYING FREQUENCY OF GEOGRAPHICAL INDICATION PRODUCTS

TABLE 4.53 a

ANOVA					
Buying frequency					
Particulars	Sum of squares	Df	Mean square	F	Sig.
Between Groups	169.581	3	84.790	63.118	.000
Within Groups	754.975	562	1.343		
Total	924.556	565			

148

Locality

TABLE 4.53 b

						95% confidence interval	
Multiple comparisons							
Dependent variable: buying frequency							
	(I) locality	**(j) locality**	**Mean difference (i-j)**	**Std. Error**	**Sig.**	**LOWER BOUND**	**UPPER BOUND**
TUKEY HSD	Palakkad	Alappuzha	1.24815*	.11756	.000	.9719	1.5244
		Wayanad	.92658*	.11796	.000	.6494	1.2038
	Alappuzha	Palakkad	-1.24815*	.11756	.000	-1.5244	-.9719
		Wayanad	-.32157*	.12609	.030	-.6179	-.0253
	Wayanad	Palakkad	-.92658*	.11796	.000	-1.2038	-.6494
		Alappuzha	.32157*	.12609	.030	.0253	.6179
LSD	Palakkad	Alappuzha	1.24815*	.11756	.000	1.0172	1.4791
		Wayanad	.92658*	.11796	.000	.6949	1.1583
	Alappuzha	Palakkad	-1.24815*	.11756	.000	-1.4791	-1.0172
		Wayanad	-.32157*	.12609	.011	-.5692	-.0739
	Wayanad	Palakkad	-.92658*	.11796	.000	-1.1583	-.6949
		Alappuzha	.32157*	.12609	.011	.0739	.5692
TAMHANE	Palakkad	Alappuzha	1.24815*	.13844	.000	.9160	1.5803
		Wayanad	.92658*	.09344	.000	.7022	1.1509
	Alappuzha	Palakkad	-1.24815*	.13844	.000	-1.5803	-.9160
		Wayanad	-.32157*	.11443	.016	-.5970	-.0461
	Wayanad	Palakkad	-.92658*	.09344	.000	-1.1509	-.7022
		Alappuzha	.32157*	.11443	.016	.0461	.5970
*. The mean difference is significant at the 0.05 level.							

149

Table

101

102

The analysis conducted to examine the relationship between the type of locality and the buying frequency of geographical indication products utilized an ANOVA and subsequent multiple comparison tests. The results revealed an exceptionally significant overall difference in buying frequency across different types of localities, with a p-value of less than 0.001. This signifies that the type of locality plays a significant role in influencing how frequently individuals purchase geographical indication products. Further investigation through the multiple comparison tests elucidated specific patterns. Notably, residents of Palakkad and Wayanad exhibited significantly higher buying frequencies compared to those in Alappuzha, with substantial mean differences. Conversely, individuals from Alappuzha had notably lower buying frequencies when compared to their counterparts in Palakkad and Wayanad. These findings underscore the substantial impact of the type of locality on buying behaviour concerning geographical indication products. They imply that businesses and producers of such products should tailor their marketing strategies and distribution approaches to suit the distinct buying patterns associated with different localities. Understanding these variations in buying frequency is essential for effectively targeting and engaging consumers in various geographical areas.

150

Results

CHAPTER V

SUMMARY, FINDINGS, SUGGESTIONS AND CONCLUSION

FINDINGS OF THE STUDY

DEMOGRAPHIC AND SOCIO-ECONOMIC PROFILE OF THE RESPONDENTS

- The samples of the study constitute 50.1 per cent female as they are identified as Consumers of Geographical Indication products.
- The study observed that 39.8 per cent of the respondents are aged between 30-40 years.
- Nearly, 39.00 per cent of the sample populations had completed their graduation.

- Out of the 565 respondents surveyed 41.8 per cent are working in the Private sector.

- Almost, 47.6 per cent of the samples earn monthly income between 20000-30000.

- About 67.8 percent of the sample population live in nuclear family.

AWARENESS TOWARDS GEOGRAPHICAL INDICATION PRODUCTS

- The awareness of GI Tag is very less among the consumers.

- The purchasing is done based on the product name rather than the tag. There is a need to bring huge awareness of GI Tag and the benefits of the product to the consumers.
- Respondents having well awareness towards More than 90 per cent of the Geographical Indication products of Kerala.
- 58.4 per cent respondents are well aware about Palakkadan matta rice

- Almost Half of the Respondents well aware about Marayoor Jaggery and Nilabur teak i.e., 53.07 per cent of the Respondents.
- Aranmula Kannadi is the Fourth Popular Product among the GI Products of Kerala.

- About 47.8 percent respondents well aware about Kuthampullly dhoties and Maddalam of Palakkad.

- 34 per cent respondents not aware about Cannanore home furnishings.

- Brass Broidered Coconut Shell Crafts of Kerala, Payyannur Pavithra Ring, Tirur Betel Leaf are the least known GI Product of Kerala among respondents

RESPONDENT'S SATISFACTION TOWARDS GI PRODUCTS

- 64.6% Respondents are Highly satisfied with the Pride of Possession and Eco Friendly Features of Geographical Indication Products
- More than half of the respondents are highly satisfied with the usefulness and durability of the GI products.

- Almost 15% of the respondents are highly dissatisfied with the availability of GI Products.
- Around 27.6% respondents are dissatisfied with the after sales support of the GI Products.
- 32.7 percent respondents have neutral opinion towards pricing of Geographical Indication Products.FACTORS

- **INFLUENCING THE PURCHASE OF GEOGRAPHICAL INDICATION PRODUCTS**
- Psychological factors are the most influencing factors in the Purchase of GI products.
- Personal factors are the second most influencing factor after the psychological factors.
- Socio cultural factors having a significant influencing on the Purchase of Geographical Indication products it ranked third position.
- Economic factors rank the least influencing factor in the Purchase of GI products, so the consumers are not worry about the price if the quality products are available.

PURCHASE INTENTIONS OF GI PRODUCTS

- Majority of the respondents purchased the GI products because of the recommendation from their family.
- More than 55% of the respondents opined Uniqueness of GI products attracted them towards the Purchase.
- 43 % Respondent opined that Traditional Values and benefits of the product attracted me towards GI Products.
- **PROBLEMS RELATED TO THE PURCHASE OF GEOGRAPHICAL INDICATION PRODUCTS**

- GI-tagged products often come with a price premium due to their unique qualities and association with a specific region. Consumers may find these products more expensive than non-GI alternatives.
- GI products are typically produced in specific geographic regions, leading to limited availability outside those areas. Consumers in other regions may have difficulty accessing these products.
- The popularity of GI products can lead to counterfeiting and imitation, where products claim to have the GI tag but are not genuine. Consumers may unknowingly purchase counterfeit products.
- Consumers may not always have access to comprehensive information about the GI products they are buying. This can make it challenging to understand the unique qualities or production methods associated with the GI.

HYPOTHESES RESULTS

- The regression result observed that Economic factor has a significant influence/impact on Purchase Intention of GI products, thus, H1 could be fully asserted. The interpretation is that, for one unit increase in the rating scale of agreement on Economic factor construct, one could expect about 0.752 times (about 75 %) increase in the agreement towards Purchase Intention given other factors remain fixed or same.

- The regression result observed that Psychological factor has a significant influence/impact on Purchase Intention of GI products, thus, H3 could be fully asserted. The interpretation is that, for one unit increase in the rating scale of agreement on Psychological construct, one could expect about 0.705 times (about 70 %) increase in the agreement towards Purchase Intention given other factors remain fixed or same.
- The regression result observed that Personal factor has a significant ($ß = 0.573$; CR = 10.991, $p<0.05$) influence/impact on Purchase Intention of GI products, thus, H4 could be fully asserted. The interpretation is that, for one unit increase in the rating scale of agreement on Personal construct, one

could expect about 0.573 times (about 57%) increase in the agreement towards Purchase Intention given other factors remain fixed or same.

- One sample Wilcoxon signed rank test result observed that the p-value (0.068) is greater than the significant at 5 percent level. Hence, the null hypothesis (H0) that a higher proportion of respondents are remaining neutral to the above statement is accepted and alternative (H1) is rejected. It observed from the above table that there are almost a similar number of respondents with a negative sign (180 respondents) and number of respondents with a positive sign [160 respondents].
- One sample Wilcoxon signed rank test result (Table 29), it is observed that the p-value (0.000) is less than the significant at 5 percent level. Hence, the null hypothesis (H0) that a higher proportion of respondents are remaining neutral to the above statement is rejected and alternative (H1) is accepted. Before accepting any one of the two alternative hypotheses, we need to observe the one sample Wilcoxon signed rank test result (Table K-8). Accordingly, there are a higher (249) number respondents with a positive sign as compared to number of respondents with a negative sign [138 respondents].
- One sample Wilcoxon signed rank test result observed that the p-value (0.3209) is greater than the significant at 5 percent level. Hence, the null hypothesis (H0) that a higher proportion of respondents are remaining neutral to the above statement is

accepted and alternative (H1) is rejected. It observed from the above table that there are almost a similar number of respondents with a negative sign (172 respondents) and number of respondents with a positive sign [196 respondents].

- The Correlation results indicate a strong positive correlation between these two variables. Specifically, the Pearson Correlation coefficient between satisfaction level and awareness is 0.838, which is highly significant at the 0.01 level (two-tailed). This suggests a robust and positive association between the level of satisfaction that customers experience with GI products and their awareness of these products. In other words, as customers become more aware of GI products, their satisfaction levels tend to increase.
- The ANOVA results underscore the significance of the relationship, with a highly substantial F-statistic of 4673.663. The coefficients in the model confirm that customer buying behaviour plays a pivotal role, with a Beta coefficient of 0.945, signifying a strong positive association. This implies that as customer buying behavior increases, there is a pronounced tendency for consumers to respond positively to products bearing geographical indication labels.
- The correlation analysis results indicate a significant positive correlation between these two variables. Specifically, the Pearson Correlation coefficient between satisfaction level and problems faced is 0.544, which is highly significant at the

0.01 level (two-tailed). This suggests a meaningful and positive association between the level of satisfaction that customers experience with GI products and the problems they encounter when dealing with these products.

- it is observed from the independent t-test result that there is no significant difference in mean rating scores of level of agreement between Male and Female educators with respect to dimensions namely Economic Factor ,Socio-Cultural factor, Psychological Factor, Personal Factor and Purchase Intention at 5% level of significance. Hence, the null hypothesis is accepted and alternative hypothesis is rejected. In essence, there is no statistical evidence to conclude that there is a significant difference in the mean scores rated by both male and female customers with respect to above dimensions.

- It is observed from the one way ANOVA result that the p-value of all the five dimensions are greater than the significance alpha level of 0.05. Thus, it is concluded that there is no significant (statistically) difference in mean rating scores of level of agreement across four categories of age group (21 to 30 years, 31 to 40 years, 41 to 50 years and greater than 50 years) of customers with respect to above dimensions at 5% level of significance.

- ANOVA results reveal an extremely significant overall difference in satisfaction levels based on age groups, with a very low p-value of less than 0.001. This suggests that age significantly influences how individuals perceive and rate their satisfaction with geographical indication products.
- It is observed from the one way ANOVA result that the p-value of all the five dimensions are greater than the significance alpha level of 0.05. Thus, it is concluded that there is no significant (statistically) difference in mean rating scores of level of agreement across four levels of Monthly Income of customers with respect to above dimensions at 5% level of significance.
- It is observed from the one way ANOVA result that the p-value of all the five dimensions are greater than the significance alpha level of 0.05. Thus, it is concluded that there is no significant (statistically) difference in mean rating scores of level of agreement across four levels of educational status of customers with respect to above dimensions at 5% level of significance.
- The results Analysis of Variance (ANOVA) test, reveal a significant relationship between these two variables. The ANOVA results indicate that there is a substantial variation in satisfaction levels among customers with different educational qualifications. The between-groups variance is statistically significant, with an F-statistic of 1126.195 and a corresponding p-value of less than 0.001. This suggests that educational qualifications have a considerable impact on customers' satisfaction levels when it comes to GI products.

- The analysis conducted to examine the relationship between the type of locality and the buying frequency of geographical indication products utilized an ANOVA and subsequent multiple comparison tests. The results revealed an exceptionally significant overall difference in buying frequency across different types of localities, with a p-value of less than 0.001. This signifies that the type of locality plays a significant role in influencing how frequently individuals purchase geographical indication products.
-

○ **SUGGESTIONS OF THE STUDY**

SUGGESTIONS TO THE GI PRODUCERS/MARKETERS

- Most GI consumers fall under the category of females, which indicates the target market for GI Tagged products. Women promoters and influencers can leverage advertising and attract female audiences.
- The consumers fall under the middle-aged category, where outbound marketing techniques, namely GI product catalogues, Online and offline advertisements, social selling, and public relation, mainly through Facebook and WhatsApp, act as the optimum way to increase brand awareness.
- GI Tagged products namely Kuthampully Sarees, Malabar pepper, Palakkadan Matta rice, Aranmula Kannadi, Kuthampully Set Mund, have higher demand in the market. The government can display these products initially in e- commerce platforms. On the other hand, Screw Pine Craft, Pokkali Rice, Travancore Jaggery, Kaipad Rice and Tirur Betal Leaf's requires mass campaigns and outbound marketing.
- Geographical Indication labels can catch premium pricing. This attracts tourists and consumers who seek quality over a deal. As GI have exquisite uniqueness and benefits, this strategy builds perceived value. Luxury will also be reflected.
- A standard competitive pricing should be determined according to each GI Product category. Affordability of products can increase the usage of regional GI Tagged products with unblemished taste, quality and uniqueness. This eliminates the chances of inferior GI goods.

- Cooperative societies should actively participate in stock accumulation and distribution to retail showrooms. All authorised GI users and manufacturers should be a member of the society. Further, the secretary should ensure the implication of tags and 100 per cent quality checks before the product is dispatched.
- Selling GIs in retail outlets and dedicating exclusive GI showrooms can increase brand presence and visibility. In this way producers can increase their revenue potential without over extending the resources.
- Developing direct buying and selling relationships by arranging state, National exhibitions, UTSAAVS at adequate intervals. Virtual exhibitions for GIs can be developed which can make the producers sustain their income even during the pandemic. Campaigns and brand mnemonics highlighting the "GI" as a brand can be ensured.
- Commerce platforms. On the other hand, Screw Pine Craft, Pokkali Rice, Travancore Jaggery, Kaipad Rice and Tirur Betal Leaf's requires mass campaigns and outbound marketing.
- Geographical Indication labels can catch premium pricing. This attracts tourists and consumers who seek quality over a deal. As GI have exquisite uniqueness and benefits, this strategy builds perceived value. Luxury will also be reflected.
- A standard competitive pricing should be determined according to each GI Product category. For example – Balarampuram Sarees Prices should be fixed according to the effort, cost of production and raw materials, other market conditions. This should be the selling cost of these Balarampuram sarees irrespective of the place of sale. Affordability of products can increase the usage of regional GI Tagged products with unblemished taste, quality and uniqueness. This eliminates the chances of inferior GI goods.
- Cooperative societies should actively participate in stock accumulation and distribution to retail showrooms. All authorised GI users and manufacturers should be a member of the society. Further, the secretary should ensure the implication of tags and 100 per cent quality checks before the product is dispatched.

- Selling GIs in retail outlets and dedicating exclusive GI showrooms can increase brand presence and visibility. In this way producers can increase their revenue potential without over extending the resources.
- Most of the Consumers are not satisfied with the after sale services and packaging of GI Products, so the producers should make necessary steps to improve packing and after sale services.
- Online marketing and Digital technologies should be used for the marketing of GI Products.
- Regional ethnocentrism positively influence the purchase of GI Tagged products, so the producers should provide the region and country of origin in the labels of the product
- The product have to tagged with GI, which enables consumers to quickly identify and purchase the regionally authentic GI product
- Marketers can highly concentrate on various functions of marketing like segmentation and positioning of the product while selling the GI Tagged products
- Promotional techniques should clearly indicate the place of origin and the qualities of the product.

- **SUGGESTIONS TO THE GOVERNMENT**

- The concerned government authorities must ensure the laws pertaining to GI must be appropriately enforced against production and manufacturing of duplicate products which are registered under GI.
- There should be tax benefits for the producers of GI products. A special category tax for GI products can be introduced.
- GI products can also be promoted under tourism and can be marketed in airports and tourists places.

- Proper legal knowledge and advice must be made available to the producers of GI, to protect their product from illegal.

- One of the major concerns raised by the producers was regarding the premium pricing of the product. The government must set a premium price for all products registered under GI. This will promote and encourage the producers of these products not to deviate from the traditional approach.
- The government must undertake worldwide marketing of these products and promote these products as an exclusive category brand which can be termed as GI brand.
- A representative body comprising technical experts and the government can do quality checks. DPIIT can facilitate this.
- GI brand once developed, higher awareness highlighting the benefits add value to the products.
- Artisans/producer's Identity cards, recognition of their efforts, Rewards, and Creation of GI panchayats creates positive behaviour among producers in Kerala. This enables a positive encouragement and enthusiasm among the group.
- Duplicated goods can be eliminated only through the usage of tags. Traceability can be ensured using a barcode technology. This creates a positive reputation among the customers.
- Facilitation of a common centre for stock accumulation and stringent punishment for those who are producing duplicate goods and claiming it as GI. For example – application of low – quality fabric in Kasargod sarees. Government should limit the production within the geographical boundary as specified and registered in the GI registry.

CONCLUSION

India is a place where there is a treasure, blessed with rich regular assets of farming items and different merchandise of high monetary worth. Rustic people in different districts of our nation have one of a kind aptitude and ability to create high-quality items like crafted works, adornments, materials other related items and they are engaged with the above expertise for a few ages. Frequently associated with customs, practices and culture, geographical indications are firmly intertwined into provincial lives which utilize conventional strategies, practices and skill to deliver these products related to land signs.

In conclusion, this thesis has delved into the intricate web of factors that exert a profound influence on consumer behavior in the context of Geographical Indication (GI) products. Through extensive research and analysis, it is evident that consumer choices and preferences regarding GI products are shaped by a multifaceted interplay of variables, spanning from Economic, Socio-Cultural, Personal and psychological dimensions to marketing strategies and product characteristics.

The research findings underscore the necessity for both producers and policymakers to acknowledge these influencing factors and tailor their strategies accordingly. For producers, this means investing in quality control, branding, and marketing efforts to convey the authenticity and unique characteristics of their GI products. Policymakers, on the other hand, must establish regulatory frameworks and protection mechanisms that safeguard the integrity of geographical indications while promoting consumer awareness and trust.

As the global marketplace continues to evolve and consumers become more discerning, the factors explored in this thesis will remain vital considerations for those involved in the production and marketing of GI products. This study contributes to a deeper understanding of consumer behavior within this specific context and provides a foundation for further research and practical applications that can drive the success of geographical indication products in an ever-changing world of commerce. In essence, the consumer behavior surrounding GI products is a dynamic and intricate field that demands ongoing attention and adaptation by all stakeholders involved.

FURTHER SCOPE FOR THE STUDY

Though this study is conducted at an elaborate scale and contains discussion on number of dimensions, still it has certain limitations as mentioned in the Chapter I. The shortcoming of this study opens valuable opportunities to the future researcher to choose this topic for further elaborate analysis and discussion with the change in the time period.

This study points to the need for independent evaluation of each GI, based on the consumer behaviour. Though there are different sets of norms already existing in the process of GI registration, the present addition will make registration of GI a more credible tool for marketing the products in a better level. Even if the GI registration is aiming at the protection of name, the basic flow of consumer perception moves in a different way. This research identifies certain factors like ethnocentric (GI) values, product uniqueness values, price value, reputation value as influencing consumer purchase decision and prepares an index for its evaluation. The questionnaire so developed, can be used for further research work in other marketing studies on GI, such as Digitalisation of Marketing of GI products, Adoption of Block Chain Technology in GI Tagged Products, Application of AI In the promotion of GI Tagged Products.

Bibliography

I. JOURNALS AND ARTICLES

- Agarwal, R (2000). Individual Acceptance of Information Technology, Pinnaflex Education Resources,85 -104
- Agarwal, S., & Barone, M. J. (2005). Emerging issues for geographical indication branding strategies, 1(4), 45 - 99.
- Albayram Dogan, Zübeyde & Mattas, Konstadinos & Tsakiridou, Efthimia. (2014). Purchasing local and non-local products labelled with geographical indications (GIs). Operational Research. 14. 1-15. 10.1007/s12351-014-0154-9.
- Anson, C. (2012). Marketing flexibilities in Geographical Indications (GI) and trademark: a Comparative Study. Indianresearchjournals.Com, 1(11), 100 -107.
- Anson, C. J., & Pavithran, K. B. (2013). Pokkali rice production under geographical indication protection: The attitude of farmers. Journal of Intellectual Property Rights, 19(1), 49 - 53.
- Arroyo, S. E. J., Hogan, V., Wisdom, D. A., Moldenhauer, K. A. K., & Seo, H.-S. (n.d.). Effect of Geographical Indication Information on Consumer Acceptability of Cooked Aromatic Rice. https://doi.org/10.3390/foods9121843
- Aggarwal, R., Singh, H., & Prashar, S. (2014). Branding of geographical indications in India: A paradigm to sustain its premium value. International Journal of Law and Management, 56(6), 431- 442. https://doi.org/10.1108/IJLMA-08-2012-0029
- Bardone E & Spalvena A. (2019) European Union food quality schemes and the transformation of traditional foods into European products in Latvia and Estonia. Appetite, 135, 43-53. 10.1016/j.appet.2018.12.029.
- Bowen, S. (2010). Embedding local places in global spaces: Geographical indications as a territorial development strategy. Rural Sociology, 75(2), 209 - 243.
- Babu, R. and Kumar.S. (2018) Exploring customers' awareness about geographical indication tagged products and their willingness to purchase it through online, JEIRT, 5(7), 239-254.
-
- Barjolle, D., Paus, M., & Perret, A. O. (2009). Impacts of Geographical Indications- Review of Methods and Empirical Evidences. 1-14.
- Babcock, B.(2015) Geographical Indications, Property Rights and Value Added Agriculture, Center for Agriculture and Rural Development,9 (4),1-3
- Bryman, A., & Burgess, R. G. (1999). Analysing Qualitative Data. London: Routledge.
- Bobbitt, L.M. and Dabholkar, P.A. (2001) Integrating Attitudinal Theories to Understand and Predict Use of Technology-Based Self-Service: The Internet as an Illustration. International Journal of Service Industry Management, 12, 423 - 450.
- Barjolle, D., Paus, M., & Perret, A. O. (2009). Impacts of Geographical Indications- Review of Methods and Empirical Evidences. 1-14.
- Barcala, M.F. (2013). European Geographical Indications: more than just a brand name.
- Calboli, I. (2015). Geographical Indications of Origin at the Crossroads of Local Development, Consumer Protection and Marketing Strategies. IIC International Review of Intellectual Property and Competition Law, 46(7), 760 - 780.
- Chuwei, Z., & Yueli, Z. (2021). Consumers' Purchase Intention of Geographical Indication Agricultural Products under the Background of Live-streaming Sales: An Exploratory Research Based on Grounded Theory. Asian Agricultural Research, 13(1812-2021-1392), 21- 31.
- Cochran, W.G. (1977) Sampling Techniques. 3rd Edition, Wiley, New York, 148.
-
- Creswell, J. W. (1994). Research Design: Qualitative and Quantitative Approaches. Thousand Oaks. CA: Sage.

- Choshin, Mahdi & Ghaffari, Ali. (2017). An investigation of the impact of effective factors on the success of e-commerce in small- and medium-sized companies. Computers in Human Behavior. 66. 67-74. 10.1016/j.chb.2016.09.026.
- Cronbach, L. J. (1951). Coefficient alpha and the internal structure of tests. Psychometrika, 16(3), 297- 334.
-
- Chen, Yu-Hui & Barnes, Stuart. (2007). Initial trust and online buyer behavior. Industrial Management and Data Systems. 107. 21 - 36.
- Consult AN (2008). China Online Banking Study. http://estore.chinaonline. com/chinonlbanstu.htm
- Cozer, (2018). Consumer's Perception and Purchase Intentions a Qualitative Study on Second-Hand Clothing Stores Title: Consumer's Perception and Purchase Intentions-A Qualitative Study on Second-Hand Clothing Stores. 123 - 145
- Chwelos, Paul & Benbasat, Izak & Dexter, Albert. (2001). Research Report: Empirical Test of an EDI Adoption Model. Information Systems Research. 12. 304 - 321. 10.1287/isre.12.3.304.9708.
- Carbone, Anna & Galli, Francesca & Caswell, Julie & Sorrentino, Alessandro. (2014). The Performance of Protected Designations of Origin: An Ex Post Multi- Criteria Assessment of the Italian Cheese and Olive Oil Sectors. Journal of Agricultural & Food Industrial Organization. 12. 10.1515/jafio-2013-0017.
- Choe, Young & Park, Joowon & Chung, Miri & Moon, Junghoon. (2009). Effect of the food traceability system for building trust: Price premium and buying behavior. Information Systems Frontiers. 11. 167-179. 10.1007/s10796-008-9134-z.
- Chaturvedi, Sachin & Ravi Srinivas, Krishna. (2017). Chapter 10. Intellectual Property Rights, Innovation, and Rice Strategy for India. 10.1016/B978-0-12- 805374-4.00010-5.
- Carter, C., Krissoff, B., & Zwane, A. P. (2006). Can country-of-origin labeling succeed as a marketing tool for produce? Lessons from three case studies. Canadian Journal of Agricultural Economics, 54(4), 513 - 530.
- Davis, F. D., Bagozzi, R. P., & Warshaw, P. R. (1992). Extrinsic and intrinsic motivation to use computers in the workplace. Journal of Applied Social Psychology, 22(14), 1111- 1132. https://doi.org/10.1111/j.1559-1816.1992.tb00945.x
- Desquilbet, Marion & Monier, Sylvette. (2014). Are geographical indications a worthy quality label? A framework with endogenous quality choice. European Review of Agricultural Economics. 42. 10 – 109.
-
- Das, Kasturi. (2006). International Protection of India's Geographical Indications with Special Reference to "Darjeeling" Tea. The Journal of World Intellectual Property. 9. 459- 495. 10.1111/j.1422-2213.2006.00300. x.
- Dewi., H & Anggoro Cahyo Sukartiko & Agung Putra Pamungkas (2017). Consumer Behavior in Their Buying Decision Process of Agro-Geographical Indication Products in Yogyakarta.Agroindustrial, 4(01).
- Davis, F.D. (1989), "Perceived usefulness, perceived ease of use, and user acceptance of information technology", Management Information System Quarterly, 13 (3), 319 -340.
- Davis, Fred & Bagozzi, Richard & Warshaw, Paul. (1989). User Acceptance of Computer Technology: A Comparison of Two Theoretical Models. Management Science. 35. 982- 1003. 10.1287/mnsc.35.8.982.
- Dhamotharan, P. G., & Selvaraj, K. N. (2013). Determining consumer preference and willingness to pay for GI registered bananas. Journal of Intellectual Property Rights, 18(6), 576 - 583.
- Das, K. (2007). Protection of geographical indications: An overview of select issues with particular reference to India. Centre for Trade and Development working paper, (8).
- Drivas, Kyriakos & Iliopoulos, Constantine. (2017). An Empirical Investigation in the Relationship Between PDOs/PGIs and Trademarks. Journal of the Knowledge Economy. 8. 10.1007/s13132-016-0386-4.
- Eriksson, Kent & Kerem, Katri & Nilsson, Daniel. (2005). Customer acceptance of Internet banking in Estonia. International Journal of Bank Marketing. 23. 10.1108/02652320510584412.
- Fishbein, M. and Ajzen, I. (1975), Belief, Attitude, Intention and Behavior: An Introduction to Theory and Research, Addison-Wesley, Reading.
- Flynn, L. R., & Pearcy, D. (2001). Four subtle sins in scale development: Some suggestions for strengthening

the current paradigm. International Journal of Market Research, 43(4), 409 - 423. https://doi.org/10.1177/ 147078530104300404

●

- Fandos, C., & Flavián, C. (2006). Intrinsic and extrinsic quality attributes, loyalty and buying intention: An analysis for a PDO product. British Food Journal, 108(8), 646 - 662. https://doi.org/10.1108/ 00070700610682337
- Fotopoulos, C., & Krystallis, A. (2003). Quality labels as a marketing advantage.

●

- Gal, P., & Jambor, A. (2020). Geographical indications as factors of market value: Price premiums and their drivers in the Hungarian off-trade wine market. Agris On-Line Papers in Economics and Informatics, 12(2), 71 - 83. https://doi.org/10.7160/aol.2020.120207
- Grandón, Elizabeth & Pearson, J. (2004). Electronic commerce adoption: An empirical study of small and medium US businesses. Information & Management. 42. 197-216. 10.1016/j.im.2003.12.010.
- George, D. and Mallery, M. (2010) SPSS for Windows Step by Step: A Simple Guide and Reference, 17.0 Update, 10th Edition, Pearson, Boston.
- Guriting, P., & Ndubisi, N. O. (2006). Borne Online Banking: Evaluating Customer Perceptions and Behavioral Intention. Management Research News, 29, 6-15.
- Gangjee, D. (2007). Quibbling Siblings: Conflicts between Trademarks and Geographical Indications and Geographical Indications. 82(3).
- Gutierrez, E. (2005). Geographic Indicators: A Unique European Perspective on Intellectual Property. Hastings International and Comparative Law Review, 29(1), 1-24.
- Mccloskey, Donna. (2003). Evaluating electronic commerce acceptance with the technology acceptance model. Journal of Computer Information Systems. 44.
- Mukamanzi Florence. (2018). The effects of ICT adoption on Small and Medium sized enterprises in Rwanda: A Case study of Kigali City. East Africa Research Papers in Business, Entrepreneurship and Management,11
- Moschini, G. C., Menapace, L., & Pick, D. (2008). Geographical indications and the competitive provision of quality in agricultural markets. American Journal of Agricultural Economics, 90(3), 794 - 812. https://doi.org/ 10.1111/j.1467- 82

●

- Marie- Vivien, D. (2020). Protection of Geographical Indications in ASEAN countries: Convergences and challenges to awakening sleeping Geographical Indications. The Journal of World Intellectual Property, 23(3-4), 328-349.
- Medeiros, Mirna & Terra, Leonardo Augusto & Passador, João. (2019). Geographical indications and territorial development: A soft- system methodology analysis of the Serro Case. Systems Research and Behavioral Science. 37. 10.1002/sres.2601.
- Menapace, Luisa & Colson, Gregory & Grebitus, Carola & Facendola, Maria. (2009). Consumer Preferences for Country-Of-Origin, Geographical Indication, and Protected Designation of Origin Labels. Iowa State University, Department of Economics, Staff General Research Papers.
- Menapace, Luisa & Moschini, G.C. (2011). Quality certification by geographical indications, trademarks and firm reputation. European Review of Agricultural Economics. 17.
- Mevhibe, A., & Ozdemir, M. (2012). Indian Journal of Traditional Knowledge 2012 Mevhibe A.pdf. 11(July), 420–426.
- Kadam, P. and Bhalerao S. (2010) Sample Size Calculation. International Journal of Ayurveda Research, 1, 55-57.http://dx.doi.org/10.4103/0974-7788.59946
- Kirk, J., & Miller, M. L. (1986). Reliability and validity in qualitative research. SAGE Publications, Inc., https://dx.doi.org/10.4135/9781412985659
- Krabbe, Paul. (2016). The Measurement of Health and Health Status: Concepts, Methods and Applications from a Multidisciplinary Perspective.

- Krishnaprabu, S. (2019). Digital India-Major initiatives and their impact: A critical analysis. International Journal of Recent Technology and Engineering, 8(1C2), 953–957.
- Mevhibe, A., & Ozdemir, M. (2012). The role of Geographical indication in brand making of Turkish handcrafts, 11, 420 - 426. 10.18533/ijbsr.v2i3.181.
- Marette, S. (1999). The role of common labelling in a context of asymmetric information. European Review of Agriculture Economics, 26(2), 167-178.
-
- Sharma, R. W., & Kulhari, S. (2015). Marketing of GI products: Unlocking their commercial potential. Centre for WTO Studies IIFT, 10, 52.
- Shil, P., & Das, S. (2012). Indian tea industry in the context of Intellectual Property Right (IPR) and Geographical Indications (GI). Asia Pacific Journal of Marketing and Management Review, 1(2), 70-81.
- Seetisarn, Pimsiri & Chiaravutthi, Yingyot. (2011). Thai Consumers Willingness to Pay for Food Products with Geographical Indications. International Business Research. 4. 10.5539/ibr.v4n3p161.
- Sun, H. (2013), "A longitudinal study of herd behaviour in the adoption and continued use of technology", MIS Quarterly, 37(4), 1013-1041.
- Skuras, Dimitris & Vakrou, Aleka. (2002). Consumers' willingness to pay for origin labelled wine: A Greek case study. British Food Journal.104.898-912.
- Veena R. Humbe, (2012). Role of Social Media in Marketing of Handloom Products, International Journal of Science and Research (IJSR),3(7),136 - 139
- Verma, S., & Mishra, N. (2018). Recognition and marketing opportunities of a "GI" tag in handloom product: A study of Banaras brocades and sarees. Journal of Intellectual Property Rights, 23(2–3), 101-110.
- Vinayan, S. (2012). Intellectual property rights and the handloom sector: Challenges in implementation of geographical indications act. Journal of Intellectual Property Rights, 17.
- Vinayan, Soumya. (2017). Geographical indications in India: Issues and challenges-An overview. The Journal of World Intellectual Property. 20. 10.1111/jwip.12076. (1), 55–63.
- Venkatesh, V. and Davis, F.D. (2000), "A theoretical extension of the technology acceptance model: four longitudinal field studies", Management Science, 46(2), 186-204.
- Yue, C., Marette, S., & Beghin, J. C. (2016). How to promote quality perception: Brand advertising or geographical indication? Nontariff Measures and International Trade, 339- 364. https://doi.org/10.1142/9789813144415_0020

2.BOOKS

- Singh, V. (2017), The law of Geographical Indications, Eastern Law House, 409-431.
- V. Kumar, Robert P. Leone, David A. Aaker, George S (2018), Marketing Research, ISBN: 978-1-119-49749-3, October 2018,768 Pages.
- Krabbe, Paul. (2016). The Measurement of Health and Health Status: Concepts, Methods and Applications from a Multidisciplinary Perspective.
- Kothari, C, R, (2013). Research Methodology: Methods and Techniques, New Age International (P) Limited, Publishers, 2013.
- Donald F. Kuratko, Richard M. Hodgetts (2001) Entrepreneurship: A Contemporary Approach, Harcourt College Publishers, 722 pages.

3.WEBSITES

- https://ipindia.gov.in/gi.htm
- https://search.ipindia.gov.in/IPOJournal/Journal/GIR
- https://www.ipindia.gov.in/

- https://search.ipindia.gov.in/IPOJournal/Journal/ViewJournal

Annexures

QUESTIONNAIRE

<table>
<tr><td colspan="7">1. Name of Respondent:</td></tr>
<tr><td colspan="2">2. Gender:</td><td colspan="3">Male</td><td colspan="2">Female</td></tr>
<tr><td colspan="2">3. Age (in Yrs)</td><td>❏ < 30</td><td>❏ 30-40</td><td colspan="2">❏40-50</td><td>❏ >50</td></tr>
<tr><td colspan="2">4. District</td><td colspan="2">❏ Palakkad</td><td>❏ Alappuzha</td><td colspan="2">❏ Wayanad</td></tr>
<tr><td colspan="2" rowspan="2">5. Education Qualification</td><td colspan="2">❏ Illiterate</td><td>❏ Primary</td><td colspan="2">❏ High School</td></tr>
<tr><td colspan="2">❏ Graduate</td><td>❏ Post Graduate</td><td colspan="2">❏ Professional</td></tr>
<tr><td colspan="2" rowspan="2">7. Monthly Income (In Rs)</td><td colspan="2">❏ < Rs 10000</td><td>❏ Rs 10000 – Rs 20000</td><td colspan="2">❏ Rs 20000 to 30000</td></tr>
<tr><td colspan="2">❏ <30000</td><td></td><td colspan="2"></td></tr>
<tr><td rowspan="2">8. Nature of occupation</td><td>❏ Student</td><td>❏ Business</td><td colspan="2">❏ Private sector</td><td colspan="2">❏ Home maker</td></tr>
<tr><td>❏ Govt sector</td><td>❏ Self Employed</td><td colspan="2"></td><td colspan="2"></td></tr>
</table>

9. How frequent you purchase selected GI product(s)?

❏ Daily ❏ Weekly ❏ Monthly ❏ As required

10. As a customer of GI, you prefers to buy

❏ Always offline   ❏Always Online

❏ Both (Depends on the availability of the product)

Enter Caption

11. Which of the following GI products of Kerala, you regularly purchase or consume? (Multiple choice)

NO	PRODUCT	
1.	Aranmulla Kannadi	
2.	Alleppey Coir	
3.	Maddalam of Palakkad	
4.	Screw Pine Craft of Kerala	
5.	Brass Broidered Coconut Shell Crafts of Kerala	
6.	Payyannur Pavithra Ring	
7.	Cannanore Home Furnishings	
8.	Balaramapuram Sarees and Fine Cotton Fabrics	
9.	Kasargod Sarees	
10.	Kuthampully Sarees on Fine Cotton	
11.	Chendamangalam Dhoties & Set Mundu	
12.	Kuthampally Dhoties & Set Mundu	
13.	Navara Rice	
14.	Palakkadan Matta Rice	
15.	Pokkali Rice	
16.	Vazhakulam Pineapple	
17.	Kaipad Rice	
18.	Chengalikodan Nendran Banana	
19.	Tirur Betel Leaf	
20.	Malabar Pepper	
21.	Monsooned Malabar Robusta Coffee	
22.	Alleppey Green Cardamom	
23.	Wayanad Jeerakasala Rice	
24.	Wayanad Robusta Coffee	
25.	Wayanad Gandhakasala Rice	
26.	Central Travancore Jaggery	
27.	Marayoor Jaggery	
28.	Nilambur Teak	

Enter Caption

I AWARENESS TOWARDS GI PRODUCT

12. STATE YOUR LEVEL OF AWARENESS OF GI LABEL OR TAG?

❏ Highly aware ❏ Less aware ❏ Not Aware at all

13. STATE YOUR AWARENESS TOWARDS GI PRODUCTS OF KERALA?

Sl. No.	Product	Well Aware	Aware	Moderate	Not Aware	Not All Aware
	HANDICRAFT					
1.	Aranmulla Kannadi					
2.	Alleppey Coir					
3.	Maddalam of Palakkad					
4.	Screw Pine Craft of Kerala					
5.	Brass Broidered Coconut Shell Crafts of Kerala					
6.	Payyannur Pavithra Ring					
7.	Cannanore Home Furnishings					
	TEXTILES					
8	Balaramapuram Sarees and Fine Cotton Fabrics					
9	Kasargod Sarees					
10.	Kuthampully Sarees on Fine Cotton					
11.	Chendamangalam Dhoties & Set Mundu					
12.	Kuthampally Dhoties & Set Mundu					
	AGRICULTURAL					
13.	Navara Rice					
14.	Palakkadan Matta Rice					
15.	Pokkali Rice					
16.	Vazhakulam Pineapple					

Enter Caption

Sl. No.	Product	Well Aware	Aware	Moderate	Not Aware	Not All Aware
17.	Kaipad Rice					
18.	Chengalikodan Nendran Banana					
19.	Tirur Betel Leaf					
20.	Malabar Pepper					
21.	Monsooned Malabar Robusta Coffee					
22.	Alleppey Green Cardamom					
23.	Wayanad Jeerakasala Rice					
24.	Wayanad Robusta Coffee					
25.	Wayanad Gandhakasala Rice					
26.	Central Travancore Jaggery					
27.	Marayoor Jaggery					
FOREST PRODUCT						
28.	Nilambur Teak					

I4. FACTORS INFLUENCING BUYING OF GI PRODUCTS:

A. Economic Factors:

	SA	A	N	D	SD
GI products are of superior quality and available at competitive price					
Products from outside the state have to be purchased when GI equivalent products are not available					
My family income does not permit to buy GI products most of times					
I have the willingness to pay a premium for authentic GI products					
I always feel that buying GI products are worth for money					

Enter Caption

B. Socio-cultural factors

	SA	A	N	D	SD
I think GI products are an integral part of Kerala culture and its heritage.					
GI products provides a diverse nature of tastes and value for the product					
As my family have conservative beliefs, we always prefer to buy GI tag products such as sarees and Dhothis					
Buying GI products also helps in understanding cultural taboos to the millennium (younger) group of the society					
I believe that young children do not much preference to buy GI products					
Traditional Values and benefits of the product attracted me towards GI					

C. Psychological factors

	SA	A	N	D	SD
GI products of Kerala comes first and foremost and a true Keralite should purchase GI products of Kerala than foreign products					
It cost long run, but I prefer the regional GI product of Kerala					
When purchasing Geographical Indication (GI) products, I ways seek out for certification GI label as it acts as an important quality and traceability cue					
I have a pessimistic attitude in buying GI products as it challenging to identify GI among other products due to increased duplication (R)					
Usually, I will visit the geographical place of GI production to get the product					

Enter Caption

D. Personal Factors

	SA	A	N	D	SD
I don't think it's realistic for me to purchase GI items given my age and income (R)					
I believe that the GI products suit my lifestyle.					
I believe that the majority of people purchase GI products in order to boost their social status.					
Most of the younger generation consumers do not prefer to buy GI products					

15. PURCHASE INTENTION

	SA	A	N	D	SD
Traditional Values and benefits of the product attracted me towards GI					
When buying GI, I always seek out the "Regional or Country of origin."					
I usually look for the uniqueness of the product					
Most of the people in my family want me to purchase GI products					

16. CUSTOMER SATISFACTION TOWARDS GI PRODUCTS

If you have purchased GI products earlier/recent times, please rate your satisfaction below:

		H.S	S	N	D	HD
1	Quality of the product					
2	Durability of the product					
3	Usefulness of the product					

Enter Caption

		H.S	S	N	D	HD
4	Price of the product					
5	Design of the product					
6	Eco friendly features					
7	Worth for money					
8	Nature and features of the product					
9	Packing of the product					
10	Availability of the product					
11.	After sale matters					

17. SUGGESTIONS

....
...

....
...

....
...

Enter Caption